Papa's Pearls

Catherine,
you're fantastic!

Diane Flynn Keith

A Father's Gift of Love and Wisdom
To His Children and Grandchildren

By

Diane Flynn Keith

Homefires Press
Millbrae, California
www.PapasPearls.com

Published by Homefires Press
180 El Camino Real, Suite 10
Millbrae, California 94030
www.PapasPearls.com

Printed in the United States of America

Cover Illustration by Chad Kubo

Library of Congress Control Number: 2012942904

ISBN: 978-0-615-66188-9

In Loving Memory of Papa

Table of Contents

ACKNOWLEDGMENTS

I want to express my heartfelt appreciation for my father, Carol Joseph Flynn, and for his words of wisdom and loving customs that provided the inspiration for this book.

I owe a debt of gratitude to my husband, Cliff Keith, a never-ending source of encouragement, motivation, patience, humor, and love. And to our sons, Nick Keith and Chad Keith—thanks for your support and appreciation, guys.

My love and thanks to my mom (Papa's wife and partner), Jeannette Y. Flynn, who contributed a wealth of biographical material. We enjoyed rich conversations about Papa's life that were invaluable to the framework and completion of this book.

I am appreciative for the support of my sister, Carol M. Flynn—and especially for providing the photographs of Papa that are featured at www.PapasPearls.com.

I am grateful to my brother, Bradley J. Flynn, who shared countless memories of Papa that are rich with humor and love.

Writing this book has made me appreciate my incredible family even more. They provided amazing memories of Papa, and were wonderful cheerleaders. Thank you Dorothy Flynn, Anna Flynn, Katie Flynn, Mary Beth Flynn, Jack Flynn, Patrick Flynn, Benjamin Bennett, Teena Bennett, and Ariana Flamik.

I am fortunate that this book was the recipient of Jackie Orsi's proofreading and editing skills, and spot-on suggestions for improvement. I'd also like to thank Renee Mosiman and Karen Taylor for their helpful feedback. I'm indebted to Tony Aguila for his editing and formatting expertise, too.

My thanks to Suzanne Spicer Safaie, who brought insight, texture, and organization to the pages of this book with boundless energy and enthusiasm.

A big shout out to Chad Kubo for the cover design, as well as Annette and Shawn Hall, for the website design and development at www.PapasPearls.com. Props to Lynne Cutler for unparalleled technical and virtual assistance as well.

To everyone who has encouraged me to share "Papa's Pearls," thank you for your love and support. And to borrow a pearl from Papa, I think all of you are, "Fantastic!"

Introduction

MY FATHER, WHOM WE CALLED "PAPA," died on December 30th, 2011, which happened to be the day of his 66th wedding anniversary to my mom. He would have been 90 years old the following month, on January 19th. He was a plumber by trade, so it seemed pretty fitting that he slipped away while sitting on the throne. I can see him smiling about that now. He had a great sense of humor.

His health had been failing for five years and we knew that his time was very limited. Even so, when I spoke to him five days earlier on Christmas Day, I asked him how he was and he replied, "Fantastic!" He was the most positive, joyful, and loving person I've ever known.

Papa lived by a set of immutable truths that he used as guidelines for an extraordinary life. He learned these truths through the school of hard knocks. He was a Depression-era street kid who was on a fast track to prison through criminal activity with hoodlum friends. He had a series of life-changing experiences that caused him to course-correct and establish a path for personal success and happiness.

Papa was a man of few words, but he summed up the insight he gleaned from his life experiences in little pearls of truth that he casually, but purposefully, imparted to my sister, my brother, and me.

While I didn't realize it at the time he said it, I've come to understand that his unique and quirky sayings and customs were a prescription for how to live a happy and meaningful life. "Papa's Pearls" were my father's simple means of conveying knowledge of the ways of the world to us, while demonstrating how to be a loving parent and a successful person.

This book is a way to share my father's heart with the world. I hope "Papa's Pearls" will infuse your life with his wisdom and love so you will enjoy the happy and extraordinary life that you deserve.

Chapter 1

"What's the Worst Thing that Could Happen?"

PAPA WAS BORN ON JANUARY 19, 1922, in the city of San Francisco, California. He was born two months premature. Aside from the fact that his fingernails didn't grow in until a couple of months after his birth, he was a healthy baby boy. His mother named him Carol Joseph Flynn.

What was she thinking bestowing such a name on a boy? She named him after King Carol I of Romania, who is credited with successfully commanding troops that defeated the Ottomans and gained Romania's independence in 1878. The king's nephew, Ferdinand, succeeded his uncle to the throne and his coronation took place the year Papa was born. It was one of the prominent news stories of the day. While the name "Carol" has several meanings including free man, melody, and song of joy, it was the connection to royalty that Papa's mother found irresistible.

Having a girl's name meant that from an early age Carol learned to defend himself from neighborhood bullies who teased him. He earned a reputation for being a good fist-fighter and the neighborhood gang often called upon him to "put up his dukes" to settle disputes. Carol was medium build, well-proportioned, strong, and quick. He "gave as good as he got" in those fights, and earned respect in the process. He also carried the charm of good looks—strong even features, curly strawberry-blonde hair, and eyes so blue they drew you in like a pool in summer. These days, kids would probably say he was "a cool dude." I think he probably was.

Carol Joseph Flynn was born with many gifts, some of them innate and some of them given by his family and the opportunities that came his way. He was also confronted by severe challenges—poverty, rough streets, and a culture that made corruption and crime seem commonplace.

A second generation San Franciscan, Papa lived on Brunswick Street in the outer Mission District, in a neighborhood of immigrants from all over the world. The ethnic nicknames they called each other were far from politically correct. Despite the trash-talking, he learned to appreciate the mixed bag of cultures and traditions of neighborhood friends.

Papa attended public elementary school in the late 1920s and early 30s. Overall, he didn't like it. For the most part, he thought school was a waste of his time. He misbehaved in class and was sent to the principal's office repeatedly. He became a whiz at arithmetic because he was forced to write multiplication tables as punishment.

What Papa did enjoy doing was selling newspapers and *Liberty Magazine* after school. At nine and ten years old, he sold papers on the street corner in the evening or he'd hop a streetcar and sell papers to passengers. His family, like many in the 1932 Depression Era, didn't have much. They struggled to keep food on the table, and Papa was secretly ashamed that he had to wear ill-fitting, hand-me-down clothes. Papa sold papers to earn money to help his family.

He made half a penny for each paper he sold. He hustled to sell one hundred papers, so his father would have fifty cents for lunch money the next day. It spared Papa from embarrassment; his mother made him borrow money from the neighbors for his father's lunch when she didn't have it. Selling papers came easily to Papa. Bright eyes, bright smile, a polite, "Paper, sir?" and the coins fell into his hands.

Papa's mother, Fan (short for Frances), adored her boy, her youngest child. Fan already had three children by an abusive ex-husband. Her second marriage to George Flynn made a new beginning for them. When baby Carol arrived he was welcomed by a half-sister Vivian, age nine, who was expected to help take care of him, and regarded him as her own baby doll. Ed, age six, became an influential older brother. Another brother, Jackie, the oldest child, died young and tragically in a car accident in San Francisco.

As Papa grew, he continued to bask in his mother's favor. She complimented him on everything he did and told him he could be anything he wanted to be. Fan didn't know how to drive, but by the time Papa was twelve years old, he did.

(Imagine driving at twelve!) Fan frequently kept Papa home from school to drive her around San Francisco on errands. She praised him for helping his family, especially when he gave her the money he earned. She often told him that with his skills and, in particular, his ability to make money, he would never want for anything in his life.

Papa's father, George Charles Flynn, was known as "Mickey." Carol was his only biological child, and he too, loved that boy! Mickey was a drayage wagon driver. A drayage wagon (also called a draw wagon) was hitched to a team of horses and used to haul cargo from San Francisco's shipyards. The driver of the team of horses was called a "teamster."

During the historic West Coast Waterfront Strike, Mickey was out of work. Unable to pay the utility bill, the lights and gas were turned off in the family's home. They ran up a grocery bill at the corner store. Papa said his mother sent him there to get rib bones for soup with a demand for the butcher to leave plenty of meat on the bones. He never forgot how many vegetables a nickel would buy, or the price for a gallon of milk: forty-five cents.

Mickey moonlighted as a prizefighter trainer and promoter. He arranged professional boxing matches that included illegal gambling. When he had extra money, he selfishly indulged in fine clothing—he wore tailor-made silk shirts and suits, a diamond stickpin, and topped it off with a big beaver hat from designer Paul T. Carroll's store on Market Street. Mickey impressed upon his son the appeal of dressing for success.

Mickey often took Papa with him to the boxing matches, and as a result, Papa was introduced to the seamier side of "The Fights" and gambling at a young age. Papa had a knack for games of chance, and a friend of his father, who was a notorious bookie, wanted to groom Papa to follow in his footsteps. Other folks exposed Papa to unlawful doings too. His uncle was a bootlegger who harbored the gangster Baby Face Nelson in Sausalito. One of his brothers ran errands for an infamous union boss. Another uncle was an enforcer for the Mob.

From 1920 to 1933, prohibition was enacted in the United States, during which the sale, manufacture, and transportation of alcohol for consumption was banned. Papa's neighbor made bootleg liquor in his garage. When the booze was ready for delivery, Mickey would put the bottles in his Plymouth touring car that had a roll-back roof, tuck a blanket over them, and load all of the kids on top. Then, they'd drive around making deliveries—as if they were out on a kid-friendly outing!

When I piece together the hints, the fragments, the barely veiled stories, I now know that during his teen years, Papa was not just hanging around with delinquents and petty criminals, he was probably guilty of committing crimes himself. He was reluctant to talk about what he had done, and summed it up by saying, "Bad things." And I'm not talking about soaping windows and blowing up mailboxes with cherry bombs here.

Papa and the folks he ran with . . . well, enough said. When I asked where he thought he'd be if he hadn't turned his life around, he said, "Prison."

By the time Papa entered Balboa High School he hardly had the patience to endure the tedium of curricula. Sitting at a desk doing schoolish bookwork paled in comparison to the thrill of his real-life experiences. He was fifteen-years-old when his teacher, Mrs. DeLuci, whacked him with a ruler for talking in class. He swore at her, grabbed the ruler out of her hand, and chased her around the classroom and down the hallway where he was confronted by the school principal. The principal asked him, "What's the worst possible thing that could happen to you? What's the worst possible punishment you could receive—to be suspended from high school for two weeks or be sent to Continuation School?"

Continuation School in those days was a place where the delinquents and really bad boys went. Papa did not want to bring that shame and humiliation on himself or his family. He told the teacher and principal that getting sent to Continuation School would be the worst possible punishment he could receive. The principal callously decreed, "Then, that's exactly where you'll go!" So, Papa went to Continuation School.

Papa said that going to Continuation School turned out to be one of the best things that ever happened to him. Even though he didn't receive a high school diploma, he learned all kinds of useful carpentry, trade, and mechanical skills under the tutelage of a great male role model and teacher, Mr. Brammer.

A classmate of Papa's who became a telephone lineman said, "You know, when Carol was sent to Continuation School it made a big impression on me, especially after the teacher warned us he was never going to amount to anything. It made me straighten up and pay attention in school. Years later, I was working on a telephone pole across the street from the school. Imagine my surprise to see five trucks with the name *Carol J. Flynn Plumbing* roll up and park in the schoolyard! They had been called to do a big plumbing job at the school. I was astounded to realize that I stayed in school and became a worker for the telephone company, while Carol got sent to Continuation School and became the owner of his own successful plumbing company."

As a teenager, Papa thought the stigma of being sent to Continuation School would be the worst thing that could happen to him, but it redirected him in a positive way.

Perhaps as a result of that incident, whenever my sister, brother, or I faced tough choices or difficult decisions, Papa would always ask, *"What's the worst thing that could happen?"*

What's the worst thing you can imagine if you try and fail, or if you never try at all? Humiliation? Shame? Regret? Unhappiness?

Sometimes when we face the things we fear most, it can turn out to be the best possible thing that ever happened—a blessing in disguise. Papa told us not to let fear, worry, or doubt hold us back. He advised us to push through the fear and make the best of any situation or opportunity that comes along.

Chapter 2

"Everyone Deserves a Second Chance."
and
*"You Don't Kick Someone When They're
Down, You Give 'Em a Hand Up."*

IN 1932, PRESIDENT FRANKLIN D. ROOSEVELT took office, and commenced to revitalize the nation's economy through a program called the "New Deal." It was a response to the depression that hung over the nation in the early 1930s. Day-to-day survival was dire and even some respectable folks dabbled in criminal activity to make ends meet. Something had to be done. Roosevelt wasn't interested in putting people on the dole. He wanted to preserve people's pride in their own ability to earn a living, so he created jobs to put Americans back to work. He implemented the Civilian Conservation Corps (CCC) that recruited thousands of unemployed young men and put them to work battling the erosion and destruction of the nation's natural resources.

When Papa left Continuation School he joined the CCC. It was commonly known as the "Tree Army," and the members planted three billion trees from 1933 to 1942. Planting trees was crucial in states with prairie lands affected by the Dust Bowl. The Dust Bowl was caused by drought, non-sustainable farming practices, and severe dust storms. These "black blizzards" literally blotted out the sun as they blew massive clouds of topsoil and dust from the northern plains of the Dakotas as far as New York City. They resulted in ecological and agricultural damage. Animals were killed from breathing the dust-laden air. People were sick, and some died from what became known as "dust pneumonia." Reforestation was needed as a barrier against the wind and to prevent the soil from blowing or eroding away. In addition to planting trees, the CCC built the nation's infrastructure, including new roads, bridges, buildings, and telephone lines.

The CCC tent camps (where the crews lived) stimulated local economies and provided communities with forest and park improvements, flood control, fire protection, and community safety.

To be eligible for the CCC you had to be:

- A U.S. citizen
- Physically fit (because of the hard labor required)
- An unemployed, unmarried male between the ages of 18 and 26

More than three million men served in the CCC. It was responsible for a fifty-five percent reduction in crimes committed by the young men of that day. Men were paid thirty dollars a month, with mandatory twenty-five dollar allotment checks sent to their families. That made life a little easier for the people back home.

Papa spent most of his CCC service time with a crew building the Pit River Bridge in Dunsmuir, California, about 300 miles north of San Francisco, near Lake Shasta. He also fought forest fires, and learned about ecology and forestry. He claimed it was the best training in self-discipline and responsibility he ever had. To his frustration and dislike, his mother used part of the monthly allotment money she received to redecorate his bedroom in a frilly, feminine style. Nevertheless, Papa was grateful for the opportunity to serve in the CCC. He said it gave him a second chance by keeping him off the streets and away from the deviant influence of street gangs and criminals.

The Civilian Conservation Corps was one of the most successful New Deal programs of the Great Depression. Following the Great Depression, when the job market picked up, businessmen preferred to hire men who had been in the CCC because they knew what a full day's work meant, and how to carry out orders in a disciplined way. Because of his CCC experience, Papa was hirable.

Papa's older brother, Ed, worked in the trades and helped him find work as an apprentice plumber for a small company. It planted the seed that would eventually lead to Papa becoming a plumbing contractor and the owner of his own plumbing business.

His gratitude for getting a second chance to build a life away from criminal activity inspired Papa to help others. Throughout his life, if a family member, a friend, an employee, a tenant, or a business associate fell on hard times, he always extended a helping hand and often said, *"Everyone deserves a second chance."*

It didn't matter where we were, if Papa saw someone who needed a helping hand, he'd give them one. When I was about eleven-years-old, our family walked through a seedy portion of the Tenderloin district in San Francisco on our way to the theater. A scruffy-looking man who was shaking uncontrollably put out his hand and asked for spare change for a drink. Papa stopped, looked him over, gently put his hand on his shoulder, slipped him a large bill, and said, "Here, old-timer, buy some dinner too." That empathy without judgment, regardless of a person's circumstances, was demonstrated in other ways too.

There was an old, toothless man named Andy who lived in a dilapidated shack next door to Papa's plumbing shop. Andy had long stringy hair that trailed out beneath his crumpled hat. He had an untrimmed beard and wore the same dirty clothes each and every day. He smelled awful. He always had a shovel and a wheelbarrow that he called "the twins." He pushed the wheelbarrow around town collecting junk from garbage cans. He hoarded cardboard boxes, newspapers, bottles, and cans. He was barely coherent when he spoke. The rumor was that Andy had suffered brain damage during combat in World War II.

As a little girl, I remember being frightened of him. Papa befriended Andy. He paid him to break down cardboard packing boxes and wood pallets, recycle some of the plumbing fixtures and fittings, sweep the yard, and dutifully lock the gate and watch over the plumbing shop at night. Papa thanked him for his help every day. He casually introduced Andy to the customers and delivery people who visited the shop too. If they expressed alarm at Andy's appearance, Papa reassured them that Andy was harmless and just a little down on his luck. The fact that Papa acknowledged Andy's dignity caused others to see it too.

As a teenager, I worked in Papa's office after school. He had built the office building and leased the office space. Every once-in-a-while a tenant's business would flounder or fail, and they'd ask Papa to discount their rent or let them out of their lease. He always did. I asked him why, and he delivered another pearl, *"You don't kick someone when they're down, you give 'em a hand up."*

Papa was generous, kind, and ready to give a helping hand to anyone in real need. But Papa was also worldly-wise and didn't suffer fools. He knew when he was being conned. Whenever any of us were faced with an opportunity that sounded too good to be true, he expressed caution by saying, *"You gotta use your street smarts."*

Papa's Pearls

Chapter 3

"You Gotta Use Your Street Smarts."
and
"Bad Things Just Don't Happen to Our Family."

"STREET SMARTS" IS THE WISDOM GAINED FROM EXPERIENCE. It's learning from trial-and-error. Acquiring street smarts is hands-on, messy, chaotic, and totally non-linear. Having street smarts can be more useful than book smarts. The online Urban Dictionary defines "street smarts" as:

Intelligence gained outside of school. It can be divided into 4 categories:

1. Getting Along With Others: *Knowing which questions to ask and not asking too many; being polite and friendly, but also being assertive.*

2. Having Common Sense: *Knowing whom you can trust, and which areas in town are good and which are bad, etc.*

3. Self-Defense: *Knowing how to fight and fend off an attacker.*

4. BS-Detection: *Knowing when people are trying to mess with you, reading their intentions, and also knowing that most corporate advertisements are full of it.*

That's the actual definition posted on UrbanDictionary.com, minus the expletives.

Papa had street smarts, no doubt about it. He encouraged them in us by making sure we had plenty of opportunity to learn in the big wide world. He urged us to get out there and take a few risks and explore urban, suburban, and rural environments without (gasp!) adult supervision.

He explained the safety rules and gave us free range to travel around our neighborhood. He gave us permission to walk, bike, or skateboard to agreed-upon destinations like a friend's house, the library, a store, or a park. He taught us to use the "buddy system" for protection. Papa said that if we traveled in pairs with friends, we could rely on each other to prevent accidents and get help in the event of an emergency.

Using Papa's "buddy system" we investigated a couple of undeveloped, open-space areas within walking distance of our home. One was the site of an old, abandoned water storage reservoir from which the water had long been drained. It was a great place to catch and release blue-belly lizards that sunned themselves on the dry-rotted timbers. During the winter the ground would become saturated and the mud puddles that formed were quite deep. It was easy to get stuck, and we lost more than one pair of galoshes figuring out ways to rescue our friends from the quick-mud.

The other site was a tiny grove of Valley Oak trees and sagebrush that we dubbed "Sleepy Hollow" because it had an enticingly spooky feel. It was its own little self-contained ecosystem that included a small running creek. It was where most of the neighborhood kids learned about moss, fungi, lichens, centipedes, millipedes, banana slugs, water gliders, salamanders, pollywogs, frogs, dragonflies, and poison oak. We'd hang out there for hours until Papa's two-fingered whistle would signal us that it was time to come home for dinner.

At the dinner table, Papa enjoyed listening to our accounts of climbing trees, jumping from rock to rock across the creek without getting wet, and handling whatever weird critter we encountered. We occasionally brought home specimens for him to examine. He admired them and (with mom's prompting) told us the kind thing to do was release them where we found them. Papa instilled in us a sense of wonder and reverence for nature.

As kids, we didn't have the luxury of options like cable television, video games, and computers to occupy our time. When my children were born, Papa's influence led my husband and me to limit the time our kids spent in front of the television or computer in favor of time spent outdoors. I'm glad we did, because researchers now claim that too much screen time leads to "nature deprivation" and is a possible cause of increased stress, depression, and learning disabilities in children.

Papa sanctioned our unsupervised outdoor excursions, which gave us a heightened awareness and sense of connection to nature. Coupled with the free-roaming treks in our suburban neighborhood and beyond, it gave us confidence and skill to navigate most environments and develop some street smarts. He alleviated any fear of free exploration and play by making sure we had the skills needed to stay safe.

Then, he expressed his trust in us. He repeated affirmations that instilled self-confidence in both his children and grandchildren. For example, Papa's grandson, Jack, said, "I have lived my life with words from Papa echoing in my head every day, 'Walk like you own the street and no one will tell you otherwise.' I was seven-years-old when he told me that and I have never forgotten it."

Papa's granddaughter, Anna, recalled, "The number one pearl from Papa in my life has been, *'Bad things just don't happen to our family.'* Anytime I have fear in life, I repeat this to myself and truly believe it. I believe it because Papa believed it and said it with such confidence. He said it as a true fact—just as true as the sky is blue. Whether I feared getting kidnapped, robbed, or sick, or what-not (from watching too much "Law & Order" or just from normal fears), I would just repeat Papa's mantra and stop being afraid."

Papa's pearl that "Bad things just don't happen to our family," was an affirmation of positive thinking that he backed up with preparedness. He taught us to take precautions and to use our street smarts, so that we were less vulnerable to the "bad things" that can happen in life. And interestingly, even when what others call "bad things" did happen to us, we didn't view them that way. They were experiences that were part of life and could be endured or overcome with the help and support of family and friends.

Once Papa thought we were well-equipped with the common sense and skills to remain safe, he supported exploration of the world beyond our immediate neighborhood. He encouraged us to take public transportation to visit a friend or go to the mall or a movie theater.

When I was twelve years old, my girlfriend and I wanted to go to a popular "Top 40" radio station in San Francisco to see our favorite disc jockey. With Papa's approval and my mom's oversight, my friend and I planned a trip to the studio. We charted our route in advance and took the train from Millbrae to San Francisco, a distance of about sixteen miles. From the train station, we cautiously walked through a gritty section of town to get to the cable car turn-around, and then rode to the top of Nob Hill. We walked down a narrow side street behind the Mark Hopkins Hotel to where the studio was located.

When we arrived, the Saturday morning radio broadcast was in progress but the front door was locked because the studio wasn't open to the public on Saturdays. We rang the doorbell and a uniformed housekeeper appeared at the door. We explained our dilemma through the glass door, showed him the baked goodies we wanted to deliver to the deejay, "Emperor Nelson," and begged for his assistance.

He didn't have the key to unlock the door, but empathized with our plight and suggested we climb through an open window adjacent to the door. Undaunted, we clambered through the window tugging at our mini-skirts in an attempt to maintain some modesty. He led us to the studio where we met the engineer who alerted the D.J. to our arrival. While a series of pop songs played without commercial interruption, Emperor Nelson greeted us with enthusiasm, accepted our baked offering, and asked what song we wanted to hear. We shrieked with delight when he talked about our visit and mentioned our names on the air. He dedicated a Beatles' song to us and we sang along to "I Should Have Known Better" blaring from the transistor radio as we made our way home.

We misread the train schedule and failed to make it to the train on time. Instead of waiting for the next train, we decided to take a bus home. We had to improvise and get information, find the bus station, and purchase tickets. We were a little nervous about being assertive to ask for assistance but overcame our apprehension in order to get home and tell the exciting story of our escapade.

It was about a thirty-mile round-trip journey from our home to The City and back. For safety's sake, we used a public phone (cell phones didn't exist) to call home and check in when we arrived at our destination. We also called home each time we changed location for any length of time during the course of our excursion, and double-checked with our parents when we switched modes of transportation. We were un-tethered within a framework of safety precautions that allowed us to have some real adventures in the adult world.

You may be thinking that back in Papa's day (or even in mine) things were different—that it was less scary and there were fewer bogeymen around. According to the National Center for Juvenile Justice, 2006 Annual Report, the rates of violent crime against children have fallen. Despite media hysteria, child abduction rates overall have declined as well. The number one leading cause of death for children is being a passenger in a car driven by their parents during an automobile accident—not playing or riding bikes while exploring the neighborhood and beyond.

Papa also believed that foreign travel was an important way to broaden understanding of different people and cultures throughout the world. Even though he and my mom had never traveled to Europe, they financed educational trips for my sister and me when we graduated from high school. They helped my brother arrange to spend his junior year of college abroad. To Papa, it was more beneficial to invest in educational travel for his children before he indulged in a European vacation for himself and my mom. I still marvel at the selflessness of that decision.

All of these experiences gave us the opportunity to test our mettle, figure out how to operate independently, handle challenges, and solve problems. It gave us the chance to learn some "street smarts."

The noise from our culture screams with ever-increasing amplification to be afraid, keep children close, and supervise and monitor their every move. That kind of constant surveillance can undermine a child's self-confidence. Papa instinctively understood that young people need opportunities to see what they can do on their own. Without it, their childhood may be extended indefinitely as fear and insecurity cripples their ability to grow up. Take a note from Papa's page, and embrace opportunities to develop some "street smarts."

Chapter 4

"When You Fall Down—
Get Back Up, Brush Yourself Off, and Try Again!"

PAPA BELIEVED IN HANDS-ON EXPERIENCE. He encouraged us to try whatever we expressed an interest in doing. "Can't" wasn't a word in his vocabulary. "Try it and see what happens," was his way of encouraging us whether we wanted to turn sheets of cardboard into sleds to slide down a grassy hill, or put on a play in the garage and sell tickets to the neighbors. He never discouraged our ideas. He operated from the assumption that it couldn't hurt to try—and that in trying, we would learn. It didn't matter if we made mistakes or failed. He understood that the process was more important than the outcome, and that you can learn from both success and defeat.

For example, Papa enjoyed swimming, and all of us learned to swim easily. Diving was a little more difficult. Papa instructed us to stand on the end of the diving board at the community pool, extend our arms above our heads, clasp our hands together, and then bend way over toward the water, and sort of plop into it. It didn't matter if we belly-flopped or not. The minute our heads bobbed out of the water he'd hoot and holler in support of our attempt and encourage us to try again.

Papa provided the same kind of support every time we learned a new sport. I can't tell you how many times I tried and failed to water ski. Every time I fell and landed in the drink, Papa had the patience to pull that boat around so I could catch the towline again. In spite of the fact that I couldn't get up on one ski, he never suggested I stop trying. He allowed me to make the call as to whether or not I wanted to try again.

When my brother, Brad, was about eleven-years-old, a customer of Papa's didn't have enough money to pay his bill. As an alternative payment, he gave Papa a fourteen-foot wood and fiberglass motorboat that required repair. It also had a teak wood deck that was sorely in need of refinishing. Papa told Brad that if he fixed it up he could keep it. Brad said, "The project was way beyond my ability and experience. Papa explained (just once) what he would do to repair the boat, and then left me to it. I spent long, long hours on my own to finish the project. Papa checked in from time to time. He never criticized. He just let me figure it out on my own. When I was done, he kept his word and let me keep and use the boat. As a result of that experience, I know I can do things that I have never tried before. I seldom resist doing a project outside of my expertise, and finish most of the stuff I start."

Brad's daughter, Anna, remembers that Papa would say, "One for the money, two for the show, three to get ready, and four to . . . ." That was a cue for everyone else to shout, "Go!" Anna explained, "He used this jingle to give us courage to jump in the cold pool, or to get us ready to get out the door in the teen years when we were lagging. This was definitely a repeated saying that I loved hearing. It was always said with love, encouragement, and trust that we could do it. I still count to four to make myself get out of bed on cold, sleepy mornings or to end a nice hot shower when I'm running late."

Papa encouraged us at every age and stage of development. When I was thirteen, it was the height of "Beatlemania." I decided I wanted to become a teen reporter for our local newspaper in order to get a press pass. With a press pass, I thought I could gain entrance backstage at a concert and meet my idols. My mom helped craft a letter to convince the editor to mentor me as a cub reporter—and it worked! I didn't get into a Beatles press conference, but I did get invited to a press conference that featured Sonny and Cher. I was excited, but lacked confidence and was a little afraid to go.

Papa escorted me there and waited with me while the stars of the opening acts were paraded before the members of the press. It seemed to take hours, and eventually we did see the main attraction. I was intimidated by the adult reporters there and too petrified to pose a question. After waiting all of that time, Papa didn't berate me for not speaking up or not doing what I set out to do, he just put his arm around me and said, "What do you think about all of this?"

That gave me a chance to express my disappointment. I was mad at myself and frustrated that I failed to get the interview. I worried that my editor would never give me another chance.

Papa said, *"You've got everything you need to succeed. When you fall down—get back up, brush yourself off, and try again."*

He didn't affirm my feeling that I was a total loser and that this was my last chance for success. He let me know that there would be other opportunities and to try again. When we got home, I wrote an article about my experience as a teen reporter at a press conference. My editor not only liked it, he offered me a paid position writing a weekly column called "Teen Talk." I happily did that for the next two and a half years.

As much as Papa encouraged us to be fearless, take risks, and go out on a limb to pursue our interests and creative ideas, he rigged a safety net of emotional support to catch us when we fell. He cheered for us to "get up, brush yourself off, and try again."

Chapter 5

"What Are We Waiting Around For? Let's Go!"

THE END OF PAPA'S SERVICE in the Civilian Conservation Corps came close to the beginning of World War II. Papa's best friend, Wally Dunn, was stationed aboard the *Arizona* and was killed when the Japanese attacked Pearl Harbor. After the attack, the newspapers were filled with stories predicting that Germany and Italy would join Japan in declaring war on the United States. There was fear and speculation that Japanese submarines would attack the U.S. West Coast. Along with hundreds of thousands of Americans, Papa was filled with patriotic fervor and wanted to defend his country. He rushed to enlist in the armed forces. Military recruiting offices were inundated with enlistees. Papa wanted to join the Marines, but the Marines' line was too long. He looked around and noticed that the line for the Navy was much shorter—so, he joined the Navy.

His first year of duty was in Livermore, California where he helped put the Naval Air Station into commission. It was where pilots were trained for the war. In off-duty hours the servicemen played cards and dice for money. Papa was lucky and won. He sent money home, and still had enough to treat himself to tailor-made naval uniforms. He attended commando training and gunnery school in Philadelphia, Pennsylvania. He served the next three years in the South Pacific aboard the troop transport ship, *USS Barrow.*

Papa worked in the engine room of the ship, but because he had training as a gunner he was always on deck when the ship was engaged in battle. He saw action in Okinawa where *Barrow* narrowly avoided a kamikaze attack. His most unforgettable war experience was watching the American flag being raised over Iwo Jima. Papa's daughter-in-law, Dorothy, said, "I remember Papa telling me that their ship had wounded servicemen all over the deck whom they had either pulled from the sea or received from other ships." Papa rarely spoke about his service in the Navy during World War II, but whenever the topic of battles or combat came up he would say with a heavy sigh, "Such a waste."

When the war ended, the *USS Barrow* assisted in operation "Magic Carpet," a massive sealift that returned servicemen home to the United States for discharge. The ship docked for repairs in Portland, Oregon in October, 1945. That's where Papa met my mom, Jeannette, who he called "Jan." As she recalled . . .

> "It was Fleet Week in Portland, Oregon, and we natives were instructed to be kind to the servicemen. Three of my girlfriends and I hung out at a special nightclub where the owner and his wife watched out for us. We

were on our way upstairs in an enclosed stairway, when I stopped to straighten the seams on my rayon hose.

"Just then, five sailors burst in and one grabbed my arm and said, 'I'll give you five dollars if you take us into the club. They won't let us in without a girl.' The maitre d' had just opened the door to the club and said, 'If you bring them in, you have to sit with them.' So, we girls went to the restroom to discuss it. 'They're not even officers,' I complained. My friend said, 'So what? They're cute!'

"We sat with them and I danced with each one. During the war, I had danced with so many servicemen I could tell by the way a guy led where he was from. But I couldn't follow Carol and thought he must be too good a dancer for me."

Their dance led to a whirlwind romance for three weeks that coincided with the end of Papa's tour of duty. He was discharged from the Navy and was transported back to San Francisco aboard a creaky old, rat-infested ship. He kept his promise to write to Jan every day they were apart, and revealed his intention to propose to her in a letter dated November 21, 1945:

"I wanted to tell you this before I left. I'm glad in one way I'm making this trip, because this trip is your engagement ring. The last money the Navy will be paying me will be on your finger all the time. I sure wish I could write and tell you how much I love you, but

I guess I'm not the type that can write stuff. I try like anything, but it just won't come out of the pen. I love you, I love you, I love you, I love you, I love you, I love you, I love you. All of me, good and bad, you got me."

During their brief courtship in Oregon, they heard a new tune on the radio and referred to it as "our song." In a subsequent letter Papa wrote, "*Till The End of Time* is playing on the radio right now and all I can say is, it sure is going to be easy for me to live up to that song."

Once he arrived in San Francisco, Papa quickly found a job tending a boiler for $8.00 a day, but continued to look for more lucrative employment. He made plans for Jan to fly to San Francisco to meet his parents and spend Christmas with his family.

In a letter dated December 14, 1945, Papa wrote:

"I'm really giving every guy in Frisco plenty of competition on being a go-getter. I've got four different jobs lined up, and I'm still looking for something better. I'm really out to get rich quick.

"This news I'm about to tell you isn't set yet, but I think it has good possibilities. A friend of my father's offered me a job at a guarantee of $100.00 a week plus half of the profits we take in. It isn't altogether honest, but its one way of getting a good head start. The deal is, he already owns a Bookie in Frisco, and he wants me to run one for him a little ways out of town.

"Jan, this guy didn't have a dime about a year ago, now he's worth plenty and has a brand new Cadillac he gets around in—and he really thinks a lot of me. But I'm waiting until you can come down before I accept. This is one of the things we get to talk over. So, now you know, and the fur coats come awful fast that way."

When Jan arrived in San Francisco, Papa met her at the airport and presented her with an engagement ring. Before she accepted his proposal she told him that fur coats were nice, but if they were going to get married, and if they were going to have children, it was more important that her kids didn't have a father in prison. Papa listened to Jan's counsel and turned down the offer to become a bookie. He looked for a legitimate way to get rich instead. Throughout their marriage, Jan provided guidance when asked, and then trusted Papa to do the right thing.

They had known each other for ten weeks when they married in San Francisco on December 30th, 1945. My mom said, "We were married for two years before he confessed that the night we met was the first time he ever ventured onto a dance floor." Despite the slight deception, they were happily married for 66 years.

In both love and war, Papa seemed to act impulsively. It wasn't recklessness or impatience on his part, but rather speed of implementation when he made a decision to do something that led him to take action. If something needed to get done he'd say, *"What are we waiting around for? Let's go!"* That was a call to action to get our family moving on whatever task, plan, game, vacation, work, or anything else that needed to get done. He'd ask the same question of his crew when they were on a job site as a way to initiate action.

Most successful people share an ability to implement a good idea very quickly. They take immediate action on their plans and ideas. They don't get caught up in over-analysis and "what ifs."

Papa taught us that the best time to take action on something that will help you accomplish a goal is always now. Strike while the iron is hot. Delay in implementation can cause you to miss opportunities.

Chapter 6

"Ya Gotta Do What Ya Gotta Do."
and
"Tell Yourself You Like It."

WHEN THE WAR ENDED, millions of former servicemen like Papa, many with young brides like Jan, were ready for their chance. The newlyweds settled in San Francisco in 1946. In 1947, they welcomed a baby girl and named her Carol, after her father. Four years later, I arrived, and in another two years, my brother Brad rounded out the family.

Papa's brother-in-law, Bill, helped him find a job as a plumber. He did lots of side jobs to earn extra money to support his growing family, and within a few years, went into business for himself.

As a plumber, he had to literally swim in the sewer. One time he waded through waist-high sewage lines on Mission Street in San Francisco. When he finished the job and arrived home—my brother, sister and I ran to hug him. My mom warned, "Don't touch your father! He's contaminated!"

We stopped dead in our tracks and waited to see what horror she was protecting us from. When he walked in the door, there was nothing obviously wrong with him and I remember being puzzled. He explained that he was dirty and full of germs because he had been swimming in the sewer.

I asked why, and he answered, *"Ya gotta do what ya gotta do."*

I said, "But how can you stand the smell?"

He replied, *"You just tell yourself you like it. Then, it's not so bad."*

"Tell yourself you like it" was Papa's mantra, and he always walked his talk. Throughout my childhood and adult life whenever I complained about something I had to do, or a difficult situation Papa would say, "Tell yourself you like it and it won't seem so bad." You may not be able to control circumstances or people, but you can definitely control your reaction to them. You have the power to control your attitude. You can be positive or negative. It's up to you.

Papa was willing to do whatever it took to make a living for his family. He valued work of any kind. His personal initiative and power of positive thinking overcame the filth and stench of working in sewers.

Years later, when I was in a nursing program and faced with changing a patient's colostomy bag for the first time, I could recall Papa saying, "Ya gotta do what ya gotta do. Just tell yourself you like it." It immediately strengthened my resolve, brightened my attitude, and helped to make the patient much more comfortable too.

Life is a whole lot more fun if you have a good attitude about whatever you're doing. The biggest difference between people who have a happy, fulfilling life and those who don't is their attitude. Some approach work and responsibility as enjoyable and exciting. Others see it as an obligation and drudgery. Who do you think is going to have more success and happiness?

A positive outlook improves every facet of life, as this story from Papa's granddaughter, Mary Beth, illustrates:

"Papa had an orange tree in his garden. Every orange that I ever tried from that tree tasted more like a lemon. But Papa would walk into the kitchen eating those oranges piece by piece no matter how sour and would say, 'As sweet as honey.' I used to think that maybe Papa just didn't have taste buds. Later, I realized that it was his combined hate of waste and power of positive thinking that helped him make even a sour orange taste sweet."

Papa knew what research studies show. People who have positive attitudes are winners in good times, and survivors in hard times. You are what you think. Tell yourself you like it.

Chapter 7

"It's Time for a Back Rub."
and
"I Love You. You Know That, Right?"

PAPA WORKED TWELVE-TO-FOURTEEN-HOUR DAYS on his business. He left for work early in the morning. He was always home in the evening and checked in with us around the dinner table. He often had paperwork to do after dinner and we had homework, so we didn't get a chance to interact that much at night.

To let us know that he cared, he would get up an extra hour early in the morning, so he could get dressed and ready for work, and then wake each of us up for school.

He would quietly come into the room, carefully sit on the edge of the bed, and say, *"It's time for a back rub."* He'd gently massage our backs for five to ten minutes until we were fully awake and ready to get up and dressed for school.

I was the only kid I knew who didn't wake to the blare of an alarm clock. Papa did that for my brother, sister, and me every single morning of our elementary school and early high school years. There are traditionally about one hundred and eighty school days in a year. Multiply that by three kids and you'll find Papa gave five hundred and forty back rubs a year. That's a lot of back rubs. Plus, whenever we were feeling low or out of sorts, we knew to stand with our back to Papa and in a few minutes he'd massage our troubles away. Papa learned to give back rubs from his father who gave him rubdowns when he was sick with a cold or feeling blue, as Mickey did for all of his boxers and fighters.

Often, as Papa rubbed our backs he'd whisper a word or two of encouragement. Here are some of the things he'd say . . .

"I think you're terrific. You can be or do anything you want in life—just believe in yourself and your ability to accomplish whatever you want."

"Your Mother and I love you and will always be here for you. If you ever need our help or anything at all, just ask."

"Don't let anyone else tell you who you are or what you're capable of doing. You have everything it takes to succeed in life—you've got all the smarts and talent you need."

And he often finished the back rub by saying, *"I love you. You know that, right?"* It wasn't just a declaration of his love, but a request for an acknowledgement of what he had said. Papa wanted to be sure we got the message.

Papa's granddaughter, Katie, recalled that whenever she talked to Papa on the phone, he always ended the conversation by saying, "I love you. You know that, right?" She said, "It brought me right back to the truth that I *do know* he loved me. I admired that he could say with confidence 'you know that' because of all the ways he had shown his love. It was a beautiful gift to know that my grandpa loved me. It was the truth, something I could always count on."

Katie's brother, Patrick, wrote the following recollection . . .

"Papa always wanted to make one thing inevitably clear to me: that he loved me. 'I love you. You know that, right?' These words weren't unique to me. They are familiar to everyone who Papa truly loved. Yet, they are so personal and impacting that it is hard to get down on paper how much it meant when he said them specifically to me.

"All through my life, I have known that my grandpa loved me because he had the guts and the wisdom to look in my eyes and tell it to me directly. Often I would respond with, 'Thanks, Papa' or 'Love you too,' as a way of just brushing by this bold pronouncement, but his words would always resonate with and encourage me.

"I was fortunate enough to spend Christmas day with Papa. It was just a few days before he passed away. He didn't get up to come to the door when I came in, but he stayed in his chair and let me come to him. He was still the luckiest at the table when we played dice, but other things weren't quite the same. He didn't lead the way on our walk, but instead sat and was pushed in his wheelchair. While I knew Papa's health was declining, my Christmas visit was wonderful because I was with a man that I knew loved me and cared about me without an ounce of judgment.

"As I was leaving, I said goodbye to Papa and gave him a hug. Pulling back from the hug, Papa stopped me with a firm grip just above my elbow. I was half bent over and looking directly into his sparkling blue eyes, our faces maybe a foot apart. Just seeing him so intentionally looking at me, I knew that I was seeing Papa in sharpness and clarity and that he was seeing me. He said, 'Patrick, you know that I love you, right? I want you to know that.' A smile instantly broke across my face and something stirred deep in my heart. 'I know, Papa,' I said. Then, he added, 'And if you ever need anything, you just come to me and I'll take care of you.'

"It was that same week that I got the phone call telling me that Papa had passed away. All my life I have known that Papa loved me unconditionally and wanted me to thrive. He was there to support and encourage me and to help me to succeed. How sweet it was to have this final affirmation and confirmation of these truths that had been Papa's refrain for so long!

"As I think of Papa's ability to clearly and consistently articulate his love and support for me, I hope that I can emulate this in my own life. I strive to be like my grandpa. I want those around me to know that they are loved and to be accepted simply as they are. I want others to feel safe and cared for and to know that they can depend on me. Papa let me feel safe and comfortable and important and proud and loved."

Papa's morning back rub ritual, his affirmations, and his intentional declaration of love are treasured memories for our family. You are welcome to carry on his tradition with your family and loved ones too.

Chapter 8

"Where's My Hug?"

PAPA SEEMED TO INTRINSICALLY UNDERSTAND that people of all ages need physical contact. From the time we were little, in addition to morning back rubs, daily hugs were exchanged when he got home from work. He'd walk in the door, and as soon as he spotted us he'd say, *"Where's my hug?"* Then, he'd wrap his loving arms around us in a big, warm embrace.

He carried on a similar tradition with his grandchildren and great grandchildren. The minute he saw them he asked, "Where's my hug?" The kids couldn't run into his arms fast enough. In fact, one of Papa's grandchildren admitted that at family gatherings, when all nine grandkids would line up to give Papa a hug, she would try to be first in line. That way, once she got her hug, she'd run to the back of the line and queue up to get a second hug. Papa gave good hugs. In a brief embrace he made you feel like you were the only person in the world who really mattered.

Papa's granddaughter, Mary Beth, recalled, "At every stage of my life, Papa was the one that I have always known I could go to and be loved and accepted. There is something so good in having someone who loves you unconditionally, and always wants to hug you, and who you can cuddle with without having to talk or explain what you're thinking. Papa was that someone for me in every stage of my life—the overly dramatic middle child, the awkward tween, the self-centered lonely teen, the questioning young adult—always needing that space in Papa's hug."

Papa seemed to know instinctively what child psychologists and researchers confirm: Children need physical affection as much as they need food, water, and air for healthy development.

Once children graduate from infant carriers, slings, and backpacks, their instinctive need for human contact will drive them to beg to be lifted up and held. They sit in your lap, hold your hand, cuddle, ask for horsy-back rides, play with your hair, stroke your arm or back, and find innumerable ways to get bodily contact.

The need for physical affection stays with us throughout our lives. But as our children grow older, we tend to touch or hug them less often. It's partly due to social conditioning. Nevertheless, to embrace your child in a hug is a moment in time when they have your undivided attention and feel safe, secure, and loved. There are studies now that link teenage violence, aggression, anti-social behavior, sexual promiscuity, and depression to touch starvation. So, don't underestimate the power of a hug.

My husband and I learned from Papa's example. Daily hugs were part of our family tradition. Before the kids went to bed, we gave each other a good night hug. In the morning, when I first saw the kids I'd open my arms wide and say, "Where's my good morning hug?" We had the habit of giving a "goodbye hug" whenever we left each other for a period of time, and a "hello hug" when we saw each other again.

When my sons were thirteen and fifteen years old, they were going to a local festival with a group of friends. About eight teens dropped by our house to pick up my kids. They all came in the house and when they started to leave I said to my boys, "Where's my hug?" They both came back and gave me a hug. One of the big, brawny teenage boys said, "I'd like a hug. Can I have a hug?" I said, "Of course you can," and I hugged him. Then, one-by-one, all of those teenagers lined up in my hallway and asked for a hug too. I'll never forget that.

A hug is a warm circle of embrace that is a signal of acceptance and inclusion. Family or group hugs reinforce togetherness and belonging. People who give and receive hugs daily have less stress, a sense of invigoration and joy, and they enjoy better health. Hugs boost the body's immune system and are beneficial to both the giver and the receiver.

Give your loved ones a hug, a back rub, a shoulder massage, or just reach out and lightly touch their arm, hand, or shoulder as you speak to them—it's a natural way of showing how much you care about them.

A psychotherapist came up with this hug-therapy formula: "Give four hugs a day for survival, eight hugs for maintenance, and twelve for growth." Or you could just follow Papa's lead and ask, "Where's my hug?"

Chapter 9

"What Were You Thinking?"
"Take a Hike—Just Walk Away from It!"
"You Gotta Roll with the Punches."
and
"Let It Go—Like Water Off a Duck's Back."

FOR SOMEONE WITH SO MUCH DRIVE AND AMBITION, Papa never exhibited the tightly wound personality traits of a high achiever. He was very active and purposeful, but relaxed and easy-going at the same time. He didn't let things eat away at or bother him. As a kid, I knew it took a lot of boundary testing to get a negative reaction from him—and even then, his response to what some might see as a crisis was calm and considered.

When my brother, Brad, was about nine- or ten-years-old he built a fort in a breezeway that led to our backyard. When Papa got home from work he smelled cigarette smoke and discovered Brad and a couple of his friends smoking cigarettes in the fort that was built right next to a gas meter!

After confiscating the cigarettes and sending the other kids home, Papa put his hands on Brad's shoulders, looked directly into his eyes, and calmly asked, *"What were you thinking?"* In one question he conveyed his disapproval of smoking cigarettes and emphasized the danger Brad had placed himself, his friends, and his family in by lighting up next to the gas meter. That question was Papa's way of expressing his disappointment in poor judgment. He valued common sense and expected it of us.

In recalling this incident, my brother explained, "I never feared Papa's reprisal for bad behavior because I always knew the punishment would be fair." Papa told Brad, "If you are old enough to smoke, you are old enough to work." And every day thereafter that Brad did not have a planned activity after school, he had to go to the plumbing shop and clean pipe fittings. Brad said, "I thought it was punishment but it turned out that I learned a lot about plumbing, as well as how to plan my time and activities and how to follow through. I think I didn't do half the wrong stuff I could have because I didn't want to hear that question, 'What were you thinking?' and experience the sense of letting Papa down."

Aside from "the question," Papa had another saying that was part of his parenting tool bag. He advised us that whenever we found ourselves in a situation that made us feel uneasy or that would obviously lead to no good, to follow our instincts and *"Just take a hike—walk away from it."*

He told us that when he was in the Navy he took some shore leave with his shipmates. They got drunk, and after carousing around for hours, they wound up at a tattoo parlor in a rough section of town. Papa was all set to get a big anchor inked across his chest when he realized the squalid conditions of the facility and the health hazard that the dirty needles and tools posed. His buddies tried to intimidate and cajole him into following through, but he simply walked away and didn't look back. He never regretted the decision.

This story was Papa's way of letting us know that we weren't powerless. We always had a choice and the ability to walk away from bad influences, troublesome people, and dangerous situations.

Papa had many unique pearls of wisdom that he shared with us, but he also passed along a couple of well-known idioms. They reflect his instinctive sense not to get sucked into the fervor of a moment and maintain a level head and calm demeanor.

One day my mom was stressed out over an important dinner party she was hosting for contractors and business associates. Whatever could go wrong had gone wrong. There were numerous setbacks and she was worried she wouldn't be ready on time. She had worked herself into a nervous frenzy trying to attend to all of the details and anyone who wasn't helping was likely to get chastised for goofing off.

I watched as Papa coolly went about his chores in preparation for the event without a trace of agitation. I asked him why he wasn't upset at the chain of events that were conspiring against the success of the party. He said, "*You gotta roll with the punches.* It's a waste of time and energy to let it upset you. You just take it in stride and do what you can to make it better."

The saying, "roll with the punches," was one of Papa's favorites. I suspect that's because its origin was in the boxing ring, one of Papa's hangouts as a young boy. When a fighter rolls with the punches they literally move with the punch as it's delivered so they don't receive the full force of the blow. Papa knew that in boxing and in life, you have to be able to take whatever is thrown your way.

When I was about eleven years old, my feelings were hurt by criticism from two neighborhood girls who let me know they didn't like what I wore, how I acted, or anything about me. In tears, I fled for home and when I walked in the door Papa asked what was wrong. I told him what they had said. He gave me a hug and told me that they were just unhappy with themselves and trying to take it out on me. Then he said, *"Don't let them get to you. Let it roll off—like water off a duck's back."*

He had said that to me on other occasions, but on that day it really sunk in. Our family had just spent some time vacationing near the Sacramento River delta where I had watched ducks preen their feathers with their beaks. They have an oil gland near the base of their tail and they spread oil all over their feathers. The oil repels moisture and that keeps the ducks dry.

As Papa said, "Let it roll off—like water off a duck's back," there was something very comforting in imagining a little duck just shaking it off and gliding unaffected across the pond.

Chapter 10

"It's All about Family."

and

"I Am So Grateful I Have a Wonderful Family—
There Are No Kook-A-Loonies."

I ONCE ASKED PAPA, "What is the most important thing in life?" He said, *"It's all about family. If you don't have family, you got nothin'."* He put family first, above everything else. He was proud and protective of his family. It was in his DNA.

His mother, Fan, was fiercely proud and protective of him. She treated him regally and frequently told him he was special. She bragged about her son to others and defended him from any perceived threat.

When Papa was in elementary school his teacher paid a visit to his home to complain to his mother that he was insubordinate and wasn't working up to his full potential. According to family legend, his mom threatened to slap the teacher for saying something disparaging about "her Carol" and chased the teacher off the front porch. Fan's defense of her son would probably warrant a stint in anger management classes today. While Papa's temperament wasn't volatile like his mom's, we all knew that if a situation required our defense, Papa would stand by us in the same way.

When my sister, Carol, was in third grade the teacher made a statement that she didn't think was true. My sister protested, but the teacher wouldn't listen to her. Little Carol went home and told Papa about the incident. He sided with his daughter and said in jest, "You just tell your teacher that I think she's a banana nose." My sister took him literally. The next day little Carol went to school and delivered the message. When my mother heard what my sister had done, she came up with her own pearl, "What's said in the house, stays in the house."

One time, my brother rolled a tire down a hill in our neighborhood and it slammed into and broke the sliding glass door of a house below. He said, "I ran home because I knew if I could tell Papa the truth and explain it was an accident before the angry home owner arrived at our door, Papa would back me up and everything would be okay. He did and it was."

Years later, when I announced I was going to homeschool my sons, Papa was immediately on my side. He didn't question my ability to raise and educate my kids as I saw fit. He didn't flinch at the idea of my going against the stream of popular culture by not enrolling my kids in a public or private school. He wasn't worried or fearful about the fate of his grandsons if they didn't go to school. He didn't throw objections in my way or say, "You can't do that." He simply asked, "How will you do that?" When I explained that I would help my sons receive a good education by collaborating with them on meaningful learning adventures, he said, "Good. Education is important," and then added, "Most schools are full of baloney anyway."

Papa was *always* on the side of his family. If he had a fault, it was that (like his mother before him) he bragged about his family. He frequently told people, *"I am so grateful I have a wonderful family."* It was a positive statement that affirmed what he believed and wanted.

His granddaughter, Anna, expounded, "I loved that Papa always told us that he was bragging about us! He really would brag about us whether or not there was anything to be bragging about, but it made me feel proud of myself and confident. If this successful, amazing businessman and grandfather was bragging about me—there must be something good and worth bragging about! In the last decade, I began telling him how much I bragged about him! I am so proud of him and so blessed by him. Not a week goes by that I don't tell someone in my life something amazing about my Papa."

Papa cherished his relationship with my mother, Jan, too. He outwardly expressed his gratitude to her and for her. He respected her, complimented her frequently, and unabashedly displayed his affection for her with warm hugs and embraces. My brother's wife, Dorothy, wrote, "I once asked Papa the secret to his success. Without a second of hesitation, he said, 'Jan.'" He never forgot to plan a special gift or celebration for her birthday or their anniversary, and occasionally surprised her with gifts of appreciation.

Once, he presented her with a piece of jewelry she had admired. I asked him why he gave her a gift when it wasn't her birthday. He explained it simply by saying, "She's my lady." When I pushed for a further explanation he said, "I've had a lot of opportunities, and your mother has supported me every step of the way. She's my lady." There was love and gratitude in his voice as he said it.

Papa's own father didn't model this behavior. His mother, Fan, waited on his father, Mickey, hand and foot. Papa told the story that Mickey would sit down to eat dinner and say to Fan, "Is there any salt?" Fan would get the salt from the kitchen and bring it to the table. Just as she'd start to sit down Mickey would say, "Is there any bread?" Fan would go fetch the bread. Then, once she sat down at the table again, Mickey would ask for water. Fan would get up and bring Mickey a glass of water. After several similar requests and responses, Mickey, oblivious to his own part in keeping Fan on her feet, would get annoyed and say, "Hey Fan, why don't ya sit down?"

My brother said, "I always thought that story was funny but I never forgot how wrong I thought it was. Papa never did that to Mom, and he would always help do the dishes and clean up. I don't ever remember him expecting things or taking things for granted. He was always polite to Mom and helpful. I guess the juxtaposition of the stories of what his dad had done and what he did stayed with me and made it okay for me to be helpful in my marriage and watchful for any demanding or entitlement attitude."

As my sister, brother and I entered our teen years Papa changed his mantra from "I am so grateful I have a wonderful family," to *I am so grateful I have a wonderful family—there are no kook-a-loonies.* In his circle of friends, there were families in which the relationships between parent and child had disintegrated once the kids hit the teen years. The parents and children said and did hurtful things to each other.

Papa felt dismay and compassion for his friends' circumstances. At a loss for words to describe the behavior or the reasons behind it to us, he would simply shake his head and say with empathy in his voice, "I guess they are just kook-a-loonies." Had the word "dysfunctional" been a part of his lexicon, he might have used it.

Even though my sister, brother, and I faced many of the same growing pains as other teens and engaged in some rebellious, risky, and eccentric behavior, we always knew that Papa had our backs. He had faith in us. His unquestioning trust and loving patience allowed us to make our own choices and course-correct as needed. Our behavior, appropriate or not, didn't alter the fact that he loved us—and we knew it. He didn't blame, yell, or scold. He never became the enemy against us. He was always for us, and as a result, he was never the target of our teenage angst. Because we knew he was on our side, the thought of hurting Papa through our behavior caused each of us to rethink circumstances and change direction on more than one occasion to protect him from disappointment.

Papa's protective and supportive nature extended to his grandchildren as well. He helped ease the emotional distress his granddaughter, Ariana, experienced after her mom and dad divorced. Ari and her father (who was a recovering alcoholic) had a rocky relationship. During a particularly difficult time, he told her at the last minute that he didn't want to take her to a father-daughter dance they had planned to attend. Ariana had purchased a new dress for the semi-formal occasion and made exciting plans for the evening with her friends and their fathers. She was distraught by her dad's last-minute decision and embarrassed to explain it to her friends.

When Ari told Papa what had happened, he didn't criticize her father, he simply said, "If your dad can't be there for you, I will be there. If he can't do it, I will." Papa dressed in a tuxedo, bought Ari a corsage, and took his granddaughter to the dance. Ariana wrote, "He was a fantastic dancer—even to the newer music. Whenever my dad didn't participate in my life, Papa would step in without blinking an eye. He always said, 'You have nothing without family.' He is right."

Ariana is now the mom of three young sons, Papa's great grandsons. She said, "The last time we visited Papa, my kids took turns spinning each other in a big revolving chair in his living room. Papa looked at me and said, 'What would you do without them?' Then, he said what he has said about each of his grandchildren and great grandchildren at one time or another, 'They are going to do big things. I hope I'm here to see it.' He was always so encouraging. How could you not thrive in his presence?"

Even when you weren't in his presence, Papa could make you feel special. His granddaughter, Katie, wrote, "Whenever I called Papa on the phone he told me, 'I say hello to your picture every day.'" She added, "To be thought of daily, to know my picture was on his wall, to know my grandpa loved me enough to do something so silly—it really communicated to me that I am valued, loved, and remembered. These are things I really do (and I think most people do) long for."

Chapter 11

"Where's the Money?"
"Get It in Writing!"
"Raise Your Prices."
and
"If You Want to Be Successful—
Spend Your Time with Successful People."

FROM THE TIME PAPA WAS A YOUNG BOY in the Depression Era, he always worked to help support his family. His belief in his ability to attain financial freedom and success was deeply rooted in the concept of the American dream. Papa was the very definition of a self-made man. From a poor son of a fight promoter to a successful businessman and entrepreneur, he was the archetype of someone who, against all odds, created the life he wanted for himself. A strong work ethic and an unfailing self-belief took him from rags to riches. The desire to provide well for his family was the purpose and motivation for his determination to achieve his goal.

His passion and purpose were clear and unwavering. As we grew up he dropped many additional clues to the secrets of his financial success.

One of the things he understood well was the value of his time and how it translates to dollars. The concept that time is money was foremost in his thinking. He knew that time is a person's greatest asset. It has value and can be exchanged for money. Whenever I came up with an idea for a creative business endeavor he would say, "Sounds good. *Where's the money?*"

That was a challenge to demonstrate a way to earn sustainable income through the endeavor. To Papa, the whole point of starting a business was to make a profit. He told me that if you're not making money, then you really aren't in business. It may be that you have an interesting hobby or pastime, but it's not a real business if it's not producing income and a net profit that can support and sustain you in the lifestyle you want.

Papa taught me that to have a profitable business you can't undervalue yourself, your time, your products, or your services. Papa had a strong image of self-worth that enabled him to confidently set fees that compensated him well for his time. He charged more than his competitors and believed he was worth it. I recall him explaining that, "If people want the best, they'll pay for it."

Papa was a self-educated plumbing contractor without a lot of social status. He had many business dealings with lawyers and doctors who had degrees from prestigious universities and enjoyed a prominent social standing. That didn't intimidate him. When a business transaction with them was especially challenging he'd sometimes say in frustration, "That guy may be smart, but he couldn't shine my shoes." The unspoken part of that message was clear to us. Always see yourself in a favorable light. Believe in yourself. Don't let others tell you who you are. Know who you are, what you are good at, and rely on your strengths. Think highly of yourself and charge accordingly.

Papa told me that believing in yourself is important for success, but it doesn't mean a thing unless you back it up with action. You have to be willing to do whatever it takes and, as Papa often said, "Go the extra mile." My brother, Brad, described a plumbing service call he went on with Papa that illustrates this point . . .

   "When I was about thirteen, I remember accompanying Papa on an emergency call that came in on a Saturday. A customer's basement was flooded. The main sewer had stopped up and the sewage was backing out of the shower in the bathroom downstairs. All of the waste from the bathroom upstairs bubbled out downstairs. When we got there we put on rubber boots to wade through the water that was mid-calf high and full of bits of toilet paper and chunky fecal matter. I thought I was going to lose my lunch. I remember Papa telling me I could leave if I needed to and then saying, 'This is why we get the big bucks. When you do what no else wants to, you can charge whatever you want. Just tell yourself you like it and that it smells like money.'

   "What I remember most is that when we cleared the line and the water drained, the customer thanked us and said they would clean up the mess. Papa said they shouldn't have to do it, so we stayed and swept and hosed the garage until it was clean. We poured industrial strength disinfectant cleaner everywhere. It took about three or four hours and the customer really appreciated that we went the extra mile. We delivered better service than they expected and saved them from a pretty disgusting job. They couldn't write the check for our services fast enough."

Papa made a point of making sure he got paid for the work he performed. He offered a ten percent discount incentive to any customer who paid immediately upon completion of the job, rather than requesting to be billed which cost additional time and money. He hired a bookkeeper to make sure the accounts were always up-to-date, and he tracked the services and products that provided the best return on investment.

From the time I was ten-years-old, Papa invited me to work at the office. He paid me to answer the phone, file, and help with accounts payable and receivable during summer vacations. The fact that our whole family was involved in the business, in one way or another, bonded us together for an important purpose from which we all benefited. Plus, I learned invaluable employment skills.

It was during one of my summer apprenticeships that a company contracted Papa's plumbing services for a big job on a new construction site. They didn't pay their bill. After the regular procedures for collecting payment were exhausted to no avail, Papa decided to go in person and collect a check from the company president. He took a copy of the contract with him that clearly spelled out the terms and conditions of payment.

When Papa arrived, the receptionist explained that the president was in, but was too busy to see him. Papa said, "That's okay. I'll wait." He sat in the reception area from 8:00 a.m. to 5:00 p.m., until the president finally emerged from his office making all kinds of excuses. It was clear to Papa that the man was trying to cheat him out of his money. Papa had enough. He grabbed the man by the shirt collar, waived the contract in front of his face, and said, "Give me my money, you son-of-a-bitch!" While Papa's collection method wouldn't be tolerated today, the point is that he was set on getting what was rightfully his. He left with a check for the full amount that day. If he hadn't managed to procure the payment, he could have sued the customer in court and won, because he had it in writing.

After that, I understood why Papa said that when it comes to agreements about money, *"Get it in writing!"* Unfortunately, you can't always rely on a person's word that they'll pay you. If you have a covenant in writing, you'll have some legal recourse to collect what you're owed.

To drive home that message, when I was nineteen and borrowed money from Papa to purchase a car, he asked me to sign a promissory note. He even charged interest, although a lower rate than what the bank charged. It taught me to take responsibility, pay my debts, that there's no such thing as a free lunch, and that when it comes to monetary agreements—even with family and friends—always get it in writing.

Incidentally, when I was about twenty, I met a quirky young man who told me that if I'd come and live with him he'd support me for the rest of my life. It wasn't a marriage proposal. I didn't even know him that well. I was amused by his attention. When I told Papa, he said, "Get it in writing! Tell him to put $500,000 in an escrow account in the bank in your name and you'll consider it." We laughed about that one but Papa's message was clear. Whenever someone makes an offer that sounds too good to be true—get it in writing. It really weeds out the quacks.

Papa's message to "get it in writing" was passed to every generation in our family. As Papa's granddaughter, Anna, explained, "My dad would always repeat Papa's admonition to, 'Get it in writing.' When I was eleven years old, I wanted a new puppy so badly that I drew up a hand-written contract and presented it to my parents. I spelled out the terms and conditions. I proposed that if I kept up after our current dog (including the responsibilities of daily feeding, washing, and picking-up after it) for three months solid without a breech, that I would be entitled to a new puppy. My parents made me write into the agreement that they would get to help select the kind of dog, but gave me the right to name the dog if I fulfilled the terms. I kept up my end of the bargain for about three weeks, then gave up and never claimed my new puppy."

Anna shared another experience as well. "While my family was eating dinner, my dad said that if any of us five kids got a full-ride scholarship to college, he would buy us a new car. We looked up at him and said, 'Really?' My mom answered back, 'Get it in writing.' So we did. We made him write a contract there and then, and sign and date it. He added in that it would be an 'economy' car of our choice. We kept that contract (each of us wrote our own). None of us cashed in because we didn't get those scholarships. But this life lesson to 'get it in writing' always lingers in the back of my mind. If anything seems too good to be true in any business transaction, I hear Papa's voice say, 'Get it in writing.' It's not true unless it's in writing! What a valuable lesson to pass down so that our generation didn't have to learn it the hard way."

Anna's sister, Mary Beth, recounted an incident with a more successful outcome. "All my life, both Papa and my dad told me to, 'Get it in writing.' When I was fifteen, I told Papa I was taking dance classes to get in shape. Papa told me that staying fit was important and that if I was still fit when I turned eighteen, he'd give me ten dollars. Well, I immediately left the table and ran to get a piece of paper. I wrote out the agreement and he signed it. I filed it away. When I turned eighteen I asked Papa if he thought I was fit. Of course, he reassured me in every way he knew how that I was indeed fit, little knowing what I had up my sleeve. I pulled out that old contract and got ten dollars—and a lot of laughter and pride for being 'his girl'."

Papa's business acumen and financial sense trickled down to other family members too. My sister's son, Benjamin, took over his father's small business when he died. He asked Papa for advice and the first thing Papa said was, *"Raise your prices!"*

When Ben worried that he might lose some of his customers if he raised his rates, Papa assured him that most of his loyal customers would pay the price for the quality service Ben provided. Those who complained were probably not the customers he really wanted anyway.

In fact, Papa explained that it would be better to have fewer, high-quality customers who willingly paid the increased rates, than to have many high-maintenance customers who nitpicked and grumbled about the prices. You can build and grow a business with customers who recognize the value of the service you provide and are willing to invest in quality. When those customers are happy with the service they receive, they become your advocates and recommend you to others—and that increases your bottom line. Ben took Papa's advice and raised his prices. He tripled the business income and runs one of the most respected and successful companies in his industry.

Another secret of Papa's success was the fact that he demonstrated his appreciation to the people who worked for him. He expected his crew to work hard and provide excellent service. In exchange, he didn't think of them as just employees, but trusted co-workers and tradesmen who were ambassadors for the company. He provided generous bonuses and annual

Papa's Pearls

appreciation dinners. One year, he even bought everyone new suits for Easter! These expressions of gratitude resulted in loyalty and respect. His team members were not only skilled and reliable, they were champions for his business.

Like most entrepreneurs, Papa didn't achieve success alone or without support. He was active in his church community. He was a member of the Lion's Club that performed many services and fund-raisers including holiday parades and pancake breakfasts for the residents of the city where we lived. His business sponsored Little League teams, and his company's name on the back of those baseball jerseys attracted new customers. He spoke highly of other people who owned their own businesses, and he surrounded himself with like-minded friends and associates. He served on the board of directors and eventually became president of the Plumbing, Heating, and Cooling Contractors Association of California where the leaders in his industry shared information, resources, and advice. Papa understood and imparted to us early on that, *"If you want to be successful, spend your time with successful people."*

Chapter 12

"That's Like Finding Money in the Street!"
"Keep a Foxy Pocket."
"Buy Real Estate."
and
"If You Ever Need Anything—You've Got It!"

PAPA WITNESSED THE IMPACT OF THE GREAT DEPRESSION and experienced first-hand the poverty and destitution that accompanied it. He remembered the bread lines at the White Angel Jungle soup kitchen near the Embarcadero in San Francisco that served thousands of jobless and hungry people in the early 1930s.

He told us many times about having to put cardboard in the bottoms of his shoes to protect his feet when he had worn holes in the soles. His family simply couldn't afford to buy another pair of shoes. I suspect that experience is why he polished our leather school shoes with such care and attention each night. It may be the reason that once he was financially successful, he seemed proud to support my mom's proclivity to buy a pair of shoes to match each outfit. Papa told the story that when I was a little girl I clung to his leg as he was leaving for work and pleaded with him not to go. He said, "I have to go to work so I can buy you new shoes." According to him, I let go of his leg and pushed him out the door.

Whether it was buying new shoes or having the money to purchase whatever was needed, Papa made sure that once he earned money he also saved and invested it. It was a hedge against hard times. He encouraged my sister, brother, and me to save fifty percent of any money we earned or received as well.

Once we were in grade school, Papa took us to the bank to open an interest-bearing savings account. Every time we earned money or received money as a gift for a birthday or holiday he encouraged us to put half in our savings account. As an added incentive he said, "If you put any money in your savings account—I'll double it!" When I received five dollars from my grandmother as a birthday gift, I decided to put two dollars and fifty cents into my savings account. I gave the money to Papa, who took it to the bank. When he returned, he handed me the savings passbook and showed me that, true to his word, he had doubled my money and made a deposit of five dollars into my savings account. Talk about an incentive to save more!

He carried on this tradition with his nine grandchildren promising, "If you give me money to put in your savings account—I'll double it." Papa's granddaughter, Katie, said, "Papa taught me how to save and the value of not spending every dime I earn. Even now, in my newlywed days of combining budgets, this sentiment that your money doubles when you put it away has stayed with me. We budget savings monthly, even if it's only ten dollars."

My sons, Nick and Chad, recall Papa's promise to double their money distinctly, although they rarely tested it. Nick explained, "It wasn't just about saving money. The message I got from Papa was give back twice as much as you receive."

For those who did take Papa up on his offer, he liked to point out the interest earned with a savings account and said, *"That's like finding money in the street!"*

As a matter of fact, Papa had a knack for finding money in the street. He taught us to pay attention and look on the ground for loose change that people had inadvertently dropped. My sister, Carol, recalls going for Sunday morning walks on Ocean Beach in San Francisco with Papa when she was little. She said, "We looked for money in the sand (dropped by Saturday beachgoers) and usually came home with an assortment of pennies, nickels, and quarters."

When I was fourteen, I was walking with Papa and saw a penny on the ground but didn't bother to pick it up. Papa stopped and picked it up and said, "This is a lucky penny. It's lucky because if you save enough of them it adds up. There's an old Chinese saying that if you see a penny on the ground and don't pick it up in this lifetime—you'll need it in the next." I'm not sure if that's a real proverb or something Papa improvised. Either way, it worked. I keep a sharp eye for dropped change as I walk through parking lots near stores or malls and I've even found an occasional five or ten dollar bill! Papa taught my sons to do the same thing. One year, Nick and Chad saved all of the money they found on the ground and put it in a coffee can on our kitchen counter. At the end of one year they had accumulated $432.67!

Papa's grandson, Patrick, inherited Papa's keen eye for finding money on the streets too and wrote:

> "One time while strolling along a walking path I spotted a twenty-dollar bill in the bushes to my right. As I bent down to snatch it up I had to smile as I thought of Papa. How many times had I seen him stop walking to bend down in this same manner? As I straightened back up and tucked the bill into my wallet, I pulled out my cell phone and gave him a call. He was proud that I was keeping an eye out and making my walk count. Then, he told me that just that day he had found a five-dollar bill of his own. He said I should keep my eyes peeled and to keep walking.

> "As I walk, even to this day, I keep my eyes roaming and am aware of the treasures that others might rush right past. Papa taught me to find value in the every day moments. Even walking though a parking lot is an opportunity and it is worth keeping your eyes peeled."

Papa also advised us to, *"Keep a foxy pocket."* A fox in the wild will take an egg from a duck's nest, move it to a new location, dig a small hole and bury it, saving it for a later meal. A foxy pocket is a secret place (often the pocket of a rarely used shirt or coat in your closet or drawer) where you keep money to be used for unexpected expenses. Papa taught us that whenever you have a little extra money left over from a purchase, or receive a sudden windfall, put it in your foxy pocket. Then, if you really need something you'll have a secret stash of cash to rely upon.

Papa shared that wisdom with his staff and work crew too. Papa's nephew, Kent, recently recalled that when he was working for Papa they needed a small part from a hardware store. Papa asked Kent to go buy it and get a receipt for reimbursement. Kent told Papa that he didn't have any cash. Papa reached into his wallet and gave Kent a twenty-dollar bill and said, "Kent, I want you to fold this up and put it in a special place in your wallet. Keep it as a foxy pocket so you'll never be without money. If you have to use it, be sure to replace it right away." Kent said that to this day, he keeps money hidden in his wallet—just in case.

As my siblings and I reached adulthood, Papa advised us to invest a portion of our savings and *"Buy real estate."* He suggested saving to purchase a "fixer-upper" that was below market value in a decent location. Then he suggested using good old-fashioned elbow grease to make some improvements and increase the value. He advised us to leverage the equity to buy another piece of property—especially residential income property and commercial income property.

Papa took his own advice, and every property he bought and sold provided a profit along with interesting life lessons and memorable stories. In the 1970's, he and a partner purchased a run down, 6-story office building on O'Farrell Street in San Francisco (across the street from Macy's near Union Square). They bought it for under market value and couldn't believe their luck. The lessees included a small delicatessen on the ground floor, a hair salon, an accountant, an optometrist, a real estate company, insurance and mortgage brokers, encounter groups (self-actualization programs), and three massage parlors. I was twenty-years-old, and Papa and his partner hired me to manage the building on a part-time basis.

Shortly after the purchase we were stunned when the lead story on the television evening news was about the city's crackdown on massage parlors that were fronts for illegal prostitution. The news report dubbed the owners of the buildings where these massage parlors operated, "Sex Lords"—and showed a picture of the building Papa had just purchased! Our phone rang and rang with friends laughing hysterically as they asked to speak to the "Sex Lord." With the help of the vice squad and enforcement of the "Red Light Abatement Act," I filed the paperwork to evict the guilty tenants from the premises, and the "Sex Lord" story became old news. Papa took the whole thing in stride and said to me, "You learn a lot working here!"

Papa partnered with other trusted investors and friends on less harrowing real estate investments. He studied for and passed the real estate sales exam to better understand transactions. He read financial newsletters for tips and strategies on investing in the stock market and in commodities like gold. He said that he would have risked much more and probably seen greater returns on his investments if it hadn't been for the fact that he didn't want his family to suffer if a deal went bad. His concern for his family limited the risk he was willing to take. That said, he expressed confidence that, "If I lost it all, I'd have it back in half the time."

Papa had an instinct for making money coupled with a drive to learn everything he could about investment. As a result, his foxy pocket grew and he used it to help others. Once my siblings and I were out on our own, Papa would occasionally slip us a twenty-dollar bill or more and say, "Here's a little something from my foxy pocket." We knew that meant it wasn't money he needed, but a tad extra that he wanted to share to make our lives a little easier. In my case, it always uncannily came just when I really needed it. Once, when I expressed my tearful gratitude, Papa shared another idiom, "Charity begins at home."

My brother's wife, Dorothy, said, "Papa would often say to me, *'You know, if you ever need anything—you've got it.'* It was such great encouragement to know he was behind us just in case we ever needed anything. I want my kids to feel that way, too. He never made it seem as if he suspected we were messing up or doing poorly, he just offered to be the insurance policy." Papa reminded all of his children and grandchildren that, "If you ever need anything—you've got it." It wasn't an invitation to be irresponsible—it was a safeguard to protect us from financial or emotional hopelessness. We always knew he was there for us.

Papa didn't limit charity to the immediate family. One of my favorite memories was the help he provided to two unusual customers. They were old ladies, a mother and daughter named Lillian and Thelma who lived in a large, comfortable home on a beautiful boulevard lined with elm trees. They had a park-like backyard filled with cobblestone paths that led to a variety of fruit trees and an arbor covered with wisteria vines. Colorful statues of gnomes peeked out from beneath ferns and rose bushes throughout their garden.

They hired Papa whenever they needed a plumber. He had befriended them and enjoyed listening to their stories about their lives during San Francisco's hey day in the pre- and post-earthquake turn of the twentieth century.

One day, they called Papa, distraught that they couldn't pay their bill. They explained that their stockbroker had swindled them out of their life savings. In despair, the broker had committed suicide by jumping off the Golden Gate Bridge. They were destitute and didn't know what to do. They had no other family aside from each other and no means of support. They were devastated that they might lose their beloved home and be forced into a state-run facility for the aged.

Papa went to their house and assured them that he would do whatever he could to help them. He talked to my mom and together they came up with a plan to help Lillian and Thelma.

Papa told them that he would support them so that they could stay in their home for the rest of their lives. We embraced them as members of our extended family.

Lillian and Thelma enriched our lives. They were incredible storytellers and entertained us with tales of their exploits on the Barbary Coast at family gatherings for many years.

As Papa said, "Keep a foxy pocket." You never know when it will come in handy for your own benefit or to help someone else.

Chapter 13

"Be Grateful Every Day!"

PAPA DIDN'T TAKE ANYTHING FOR GRANTED. He was self-reliant but drew strength and fortitude from his faith and belief in God. He expressed his gratitude for his life, his family, and the blessings he received through silent prayer and meditation every day as he exercised or went for a morning walk. At family gatherings he frequently exclaimed, "We are so lucky. We have so much. *Be grateful every day!*"

As a child, I never thought of Papa as particularly religious. He was raised as a Catholic but was not outwardly zealous about it. Since my mom wasn't raised with any specific religious belief, she deferred to Papa's preference to raise his children as Catholics. We dutifully went to church on most Sundays, but Papa never received communion.

It wasn't until my sister's wedding day that I understood why. He and my mother practiced birth control. Since the church did not approve of birth control, Papa felt it was morally wrong to defy church tenets and still receive the sacrament.

That all changed when a maverick priest (that some might call blasphemous) who performed my sister's wedding ceremony, told Papa that birth control was a matter between him and God. He said that if Papa felt right with God, he should receive communion at his daughter's wedding, which he did.

That turning point freed Papa to more openly express his faith. He told us, "I pray for our family every day when I take my walk. I pray that everyone is healthy and happy and has what they need." One time Papa told me, "I pray because I want God to know I'm around, so when He starts passing things out—I get some." He laughed, but I'm not entirely sure he was just kidding.

Papa carried rosary beads in his pocket that helped him track his prayers on his daily walk. People of many faiths use rosary or prayer beads as an aid in saying repeated prayers, chants, and meditations. For Papa, making a connection with and expressing gratitude to a divine source through repetitive prayer was both meaningful and powerful.

Papa also expressed his gratitude to his family and friends. He appreciated all of the people in his life and took the time to say "thank you" at every opportunity. This was never more apparent to me than near the end of his life. He had grown frail. He had a clogged artery and was told it would lead to heart failure. He didn't want surgery, and it wasn't recommended for a man of his age. He got dizzy when he walked and fell numerous times. Papa was also diagnosed with Alzheimer's, but despite short-term memory loss and bouts of dementia, he had times of remarkable clarity. He spent the majority of his days sitting in his lounge chair snoozing. At almost ninety-years-old, his body was wearing out.

For someone who had been so active, this decline wasn't the way he would've chosen to spend the last years of his life. He was so fiercely independent that you would think relying on a caregiver for assistance with grooming, walking, fixing a meal, and other daily needs would be a difficult adjustment. But he rarely complained. In fact, he consistently praised the aide who helped him and expressed his gratefulness to her every day. Each time I visited him he complimented his care provider saying, "She's the best. They don't make 'em like her anymore. I don't know what I'd do without her." His sincere and genuine gratitude endeared him to her heart forever too.

Papa's belief in God gave him peace, strength, courage, and hope—and he believed it was the wellspring of the many blessings he received. It was the reason he told us, *"Be grateful every day!"*

Chapter 14

"You Gotta Exercise Every Day."

PAPA LIKED TO STAY IN SHAPE. He walked every day. For over fifty years he worked out with weights daily, as well. He was ahead of his time in terms of recognizing the benefits of physical fitness and making exercise a daily habit. I wondered where he got the motivation to make exercise part of his busy routine and suspected it was fostered in his youth watching boxers train in the ring. When I asked, his answer surprised me and made me laugh. He said, "That could be part of it, but I just wanted to look good."

During that conversation my mom shed some light on the subject. She said that Papa's mother flattered him constantly. "She told him that he was beautiful and he believed it." Papa chimed in, "Exactly! I wanted to keep my good looks. People are always looking at you and sizing you up based on your looks. Being healthy and staying in shape is an advantage in life and in business. To stay in shape, *you gotta exercise every day.*"

Even though Papa had a predilection for physical fitness, like many of his generation, he smoked cigarettes. His chain-smoking resulted in a chronic sore throat. Papa quit smoking cold-turkey in 1957, seven years before the Surgeon General of the United States released a report about the dangers of cigarette smoking, and eight years before Congress passed the Cigarette Labeling and Advertising Act that required cigarette packs to carry the warning, "Cigarettes may be hazardous to your health." To kick the habit, Papa replaced cigarettes with gum and used to stroke his jaw in recollection of how sore it was from all that chewing!

In 1959, at the age of thirty-seven and two years after he quit smoking, Papa was diagnosed with a rare cancer of the parotid gland. The largest of the salivary glands, it is located in the cheek in front of the ear. It produces saliva that aids in digestion. While the exact cause is unknown, there are certain risks associated with getting salivary gland cancer including exposure to cancerous substances in the workplace.

Papa was exposed to many carcinogens in his line of work including lead, nickel alloys, silica, and asbestos. One rainy afternoon, as he was repairing a pipe, a lead pot exploded embedding bits of lead under the skin in his face and neck and coating his teeth. He didn't seek medical attention. The lead eventually wore off of his teeth and the small lead pellets worked their way out of his skin. My mom speculated that Papa's cancer could have been a result of that incident.

Whatever the reason, the recommended treatment for Papa's cancer was surgery to remove the salivary gland. Because the cancer was in the early stages, Papa didn't need radiation and chemotherapy. But the loss of his parotid gland in his right cheek meant that whenever he ate foods that stimulated the salivary gland (for example, dill pickles), his body compensated and the right side of his face would break out in a profuse sweat. Papa frequently had to mop the right side of his face with a handkerchief while he ate tangy or tart foods including his favorite—a mixed green salad with oil and vinegar dressing.

My sister Carol remembered another side effect of Papa's surgery:

"Prior to surgery, Papa had a distinctive and very loud whistle that he used to get people's attention. He used it to call us home at night during the summer. Wherever we were in the neighborhood, when we heard his whistle we knew it was time to come home. After the surgery, he was cancer-free, but he couldn't whistle. The guys at the plumbing shop presented him with a gift. When he opened it, inside the box was every type of whistle you could imagine! We had a lot of fun with all of those whistles. But what I remember most is that Papa practiced and practiced whistling until he finally got his whistle back. "

That same resolve and determination to overcome his whistling handicap, is what Papa believes helped him overcome cancer. He said that when he learned he had cancer, he took the doctor's advice. He also focused on eliminating the cancer from his body. He would imagine his body cancer-free and see himself well and healthy. Papa said, "I just set my mind to it."

When I asked Papa who he confided in for emotional support when he learned he had cancer he said, "Your mother is my best friend. I confided in her. I also prayed to God for help."

Papa's life was a demonstration of his belief that daily exercise, the power of positive thinking, support from family, and meditation and prayer helps maintain a healthy body, mind, and spirit.

Chapter 15

"Life Is Too Short. Relax. Take a Little Time Off."

PAPA WORKED HARD, put in long hours, and was constantly in motion even in his seventies and early eighties. He was proud of his active lifestyle and used to quip, "At my age, if you stop moving, they throw dirt on you." But he always took time to recharge his batteries and never forgot how to play. When my sister, brother, and I were little it was easy to engage him in horsy-back rides and impromptu wrestling matches. He enjoyed puzzles and card games and taught us how to play "Casino," "Kings In The Corner," and a variety of "Solitaire" games that we played side-by-side. He taught us to play dice games too.

Papa enjoyed collecting things. He was a collector all of his life. Sorting through his collections was a favorite pastime. He lamented the fact that his mother disposed of his baseball card collection while he was in the Navy. (She thought it was junk and didn't know it had monetary and sentimental value.) His more extensive collections included brass hotel keys, decorative whiskey decanters, corks from wine bottles, antique tools, jokers from card decks, and coins. Through casual explorations of his collections he fostered relationships with people.

Papa's enthusiasm for coin collecting turned my husband, Cliff, and our sons, Nick and Chad, into numismatists. They spent fun-filled hours with Papa estimating the value of his collection using the coin "Blue Book." Its complete title is *Handbook of United States Coins Blue Book*, and is updated and published annually by Whitman Books. It's the acknowledged guide to wholesale prices for U.S. coins, and coin collectors use it to figure out what a coin dealer would likely pay for their coins. The kids would get so excited when they discovered a coin that was worth more than its face value, and Papa would praise them for their persistence in finding a "good" or "fine" coin among the vast assortment of circulated pennies, nickels, dimes, quarters, half dollars, and silver dollars.

Papa's granddaughter, Mary Beth, was infatuated with coin-collecting too, and remembered: "Papa and I used to sit for hours at the kitchen table with two huge magnifying glasses and piles of coins. I saved up coins in my Minnie Mouse coin purse and then would bring them to Papa to see if there were any collectables among them. He would bring out his own box of coins and we would wade through it all. Papa's collection had very valuable, mint-condition pieces, but he would still get excited when I found a used wheat stalk penny or a drummer boy quarter. He would label what I found and put it on the shelf with his valuable collection. Regardless of how much something cost, Papa lived out for me that value is something entirely different. Value is in the appraisal and in discovery and in relationship."

Papa encouraged us to start collections of things that we found interesting. My mom collected dinner bells, and Belleek and Lladro porcelain. My sister had an extensive collection of horse figurines. My brother collected matchbook covers, baseball cards, and marbles. I collected big, costume jewelry dinner rings. The prize piece in my collection was a replica of a "poison ring" that had a hidden container under the large pearl in the setting. It was said that in medieval times, the wearer would put poison in the ring's container and then stealthily slip it into an enemy's food or drink.

One day, as Papa admired the ring, he told me that because I was born in June, the pearl was my birthstone. He told me it was one of his favorite gemstones and spun a tale of how a pearl is a miracle of nature. It starts out as a grain of sand in an oyster that is a source of irritation and discomfort. But the oyster covers the grain of sand in a coating that eases the inflammation and eventually becomes a beautiful pearl. He said, "It takes a bad situation and makes it better."

Papa told me that a person's birthstone brings them good fortune when they wear it, but only if the gem is real. He asked me if I knew how to tell if a pearl is real or fake. He instructed me to rub the pearl gently against my eye tooth. He explained that if it feels gritty or sandy, it is real. If it feels smooth, then it's fake. I rubbed every pearl on every ring in my collection against my tooth and none of them were gritty. There wasn't a real pearl in the bunch. I was disheartened, but Papa said not to worry. He promised that I would have real pearls someday.

He kept his promise. On my sixteenth birthday he gave me a strand of pearls—and every pearl on that necklace passed the "eye tooth test."

Papa could turn any activity into an amusement or fun adventure. We often took long Sunday drives that led to unexpected diversions to places off the beaten path. The change of scenery did us all good. During the holiday season when the stress of decorating, making and buying gifts, and all of the social demands got to be too much my mom would load us into the station wagon, and Papa would act like a tour guide as he drove through neighborhoods, pointing out Christmas lights and holiday decorations. We'd all "ooh" and "aah" at the spectacle. The change of routine alleviated the tension and helped us all relax.

In those days, drive-in movies were all the rage, and I saw many double features nestled in the back seat of the family car with my sister and brother. We kids would inevitably fall asleep on the way home. When we got home, instead of waking us up, Papa would carry each of us from the car to our beds and tuck us in for the night. Sometimes I'd pretend to be asleep just so Papa would pick me up and carry me. Once I was in bed, I'd open my eyes and request a "mummy tuck." He'd tuck the covers very tightly around my body so it sort of resembled an Egyptian mummy. That playful way of tucking me in made me feel safe, snug, and secure.

When I was in elementary school and we couldn't afford big family vacations, my mom would arrange a weekend getaway to an inexpensive motel in a neighboring city. We'd head to our mini-vacation destination after school on Friday and, after spending most of the weekend in the motel pool with Papa, we'd come home exhausted from the fun on Sunday afternoon. Those little budget-friendly breaks in routine were refreshing, bonded our family together, and created many lasting memories.

When I was in middle school we were introduced to snow skiing by some friends of the family who had a cabin near Lake Tahoe. We had a blast sharing the cabin with our friends, cooking meals together, and learning to ski. Papa had fun on the slopes, too, which led to several more weekend ski trips that year, one of which was particularly memorable.

On a rainy Friday afternoon in February, after loading our snow gear into the station wagon, we headed toward the mountains. In those days we didn't have CD players or iPods, so we listened to the radio until we lost the signal about an hour into our trip. From that point on we knew the drill to pass the time: songs, games, storytelling, and conversation.

As we drove to a higher elevation, it began to snow. Within a short distance the mounting snow made the two-lane highway treacherous. We stopped to put chains on the car and continued to our destination, although traffic was moving at a snail's pace. By 7:00 p.m. it was dark, and visibility worsened as we approached the mountain summit. Papa had to use the taillights of the car in front of him to guide our car along the road. Suddenly the freezing cold wind snapped the windshield wiper off the driver's side of the window. There was no place to pull over on the narrow mountain road, which was bounded by the craggy mountain face on one side and a steep cliff on the other.

Our car, previously filled with laughter and conversation, became very quiet. It was understood that Papa needed to concentrate as he rolled down the window and tried to use his gloved hand to wipe away the blinding snow and maneuver the car over the summit and down the other side of the mountain. My sister asked my mom what we should do. "Pray," she whispered.

While winding our way down the mountain, Papa spotted a turnout. He stopped and rigged a tree branch to use as a windshield wiper so that he could see the road. In spite of the driving snow, we all got out of the car to stretch.

My brother noticed something near a small, ice-covered pond by the side of the road. It was a duck, and it looked half frozen. Feeling sorry for the creature, he picked it up and asked Papa if he could care for it until we could get it to an animal shelter. My mother welcomed the diversion, and the duck was soon tucked beneath a blanket on my brother's lap as we continued on our perilous journey.

Near the bottom of the mountain my brother broke the prayer-filled silence and whined, "Ooooh, the duck pooped on me." My mom shined a flashlight beam on his lap. The duck stood up, quacked, hopped to the front seat and flew out of Papa's snow-encrusted open window. We were all stunned and even more surprised when my brother said, "Hey, the duck laid an egg," and held it up for all of us to see.

In a moment of fear-filled anxiety when we worried we might die before reaching our destination, that duck laid a message of hope right in my brother's lap. We burst out laughing, and within minutes Papa turned down the road that led to our rented cabin. We got out of the car and hugged one another in relief—happy to be alive and together.

While we had many memorable family vacations, Papa made room for grown-up recreation time too. He and my mom hosted dinner parties for their friends and business associates and had a robust and active social life. They enjoyed everything from casual picnics to formal dances and, based on our family photo album, they had a weakness for costume parties. They traveled to business conventions and usually extended their stay for a little rest and relaxation. It provided a respite from business as usual, revitalized their spirits, and rekindled their loving relationship.

When my husband and I were in the throes of raising children, working, and running our own businesses, we were stressed out from all of the responsibility and just sort of going through the motions. One day, on my way to an appointment, I dropped the kids off at Papa's house. He and my mom had offered to baby-sit. I was in a hurry and feeling tense and frazzled. Papa said, "When's the last time you had a vacation?" I scoffed at the idea and said, "I'm too busy." Papa looked at me and said, *"Life is too short. Relax. Take a little time off."*

He proceeded to tell me it would do me a world of good, improve my outlook, and help me to understand what was really important. The sincerity and concern with which he said it really gave me pause. I took his advice and planned a family vacation. The change in environment and routine not only reenergized me, it lifted the spirits of my husband and children too. We made a point to take Papa's advice and schedule "a little time off" regularly thereafter.

Papa's playful spirit is a testament to an emerging body of scientific knowledge about the transformative power of human play. Dr. Stuart Brown, a physician and founder of the National Institute for Play (NIFP), reports that human play, or "pleasurable, purposeless activity," promotes trust, optimism, empathy, cooperation, creativity, learning, productivity, and adaptability to life's complications and stressful situations.

Papa knew instinctively to take some time off to play with family and friends. Give yourself permission to play with the joy and abandonment of childhood. Like Papa, you'll receive multiple benefits including improvement in your physical and mental health, and harmony in your family relationships.

Chapter 16

"Doodle-lee Do It!"

PAPA MAINTAINED A LIGHTNESS OF BEING. He was fun-loving, had a great sense of humor, and engaged in bouts of silliness. Right up until the time he was in his early 70's he would be walking along and then impulsively jump up in the air and click his heels together. It was a little dance of joy—and Papa loved to dance! He and my mom cut a mean rug and were renown in their circle of friends as great dance partners.

Papa taught my sister and me how to dance by letting us stand on the top of his feet as he danced the steps to the foxtrot, waltz, and cha-cha. If music was playing, Papa was moving to it. He loved the big band sounds of the 1940s and crooners like Frank Sinatra and Tony Bennett. When Barbra Streisand delivered her breakout Broadway performance as Fanny Brice in *Funny Girl* in 1964, Papa bought the album and every one of her albums thereafter. He and my mom really enjoyed musical theater and took the whole family to popular productions.

Papa installed an intercom system in our house so he could pipe music (or the San Francisco Giants' baseball game) into every room. He loved listening to music. He grew up listening to his mother's player piano. It had been an indulgent purchase, but she managed to scrape together the payments of fifty cents per week until it was paid-in-full. The entertainment it brought to their family and friends was worth its weight in gold. Papa was disheartened when his father sold the piano after Fan died.

When I was ten years old, destiny brought Papa the opportunity to purchase an old player piano from a customer who was moving and didn't want it anymore. It came with over one hundred music scrolls. We kids would gleefully pump the foot pedals and adjust the tempo as the piano sprang into action and the keys magically played an assortment of oldies but goodies from bygone eras. Everyone would sing along, trying to follow the lyrics that were printed on the scrolls. Papa's favorite song was a little ditty from 1948 called "Doodle Doo Do" by Ken Griffin. We'd play that song over and over again, and eventually, Papa memorized the lyrics★ that go like this . . .

Please play for me, that sweet melody
Called Doodle-lee Do, Doodle-lee Do
I like the rest, but what I like best
Is Doodle-lee Do, Doodle-lee Do
It's the simplest thing, there's nothing much to it
Don't have to sing, just Doodle-lee Do it
I love it so, wherever I go
I Doodle-lee, Doodle-lee Do

★ You can listen to the song at: www.PapasPearls.com

There was something about the old-fashioned upbeat melody and cheerful lyrics that just made you feel good when you heard it. It became an anthem for Papa. Sometimes, as he walked down the hallway of our home, he'd poke his head in my room and sing the first two bars as a way to say, "Hi! How are you doing?" I'd always respond by singing the next two bars with him. It gave us a happier outlook as we carried on with the day.

When Papa walked into his office and things were tense or somber or just plain boring, he'd look at his staff and with a big grin pronounce, *"Doodle-lee do it!"* It was sometimes accompanied by a quick little dance step. It was a playful way to lighten the mood. Being silly was part of Papa's personality. It balanced his more serious business side and made life a lot more interesting.

By the time he was forty, Papa had a full head of prematurely white hair. He said he didn't mind because, "It makes my Lake-Louise-blue-eyes stand out." They twinkled as he said it. That shock of white hair caught people's attention. Papa was a sharp dresser and as his sister Vivian said, "He always looks like ready cash." He wore sunglasses that partially disguised his face, drawing attention to his bright white hair. When he and my mom took trips to plumbing conventions in Los Angeles or Las Vegas, people would mistake him for the actor Lloyd Bridges from the television series *Sea Hunt*, or Lorne Green from *Bonanza*, or Paul Newman (after Newman turned 60 or so). He always played along with a straight face, and even signed a couple of random requests for an autograph.

His mischievous fondness to play-act and pretend to be someone he wasn't reached a pinnacle at an Arts and Wine Festival in 1983. Papa and I were strolling through the fairgrounds when we spotted the booth of a wine vintner whose Chardonnay we wanted to try. As we stepped up to the booth, Papa read the sign that said, "1 Glass of Chardonnay—$2.00." Papa paid four dollars and we placed our festival wine glasses on the counter. The woman in the booth poured a scanty half glass of wine into each. I reached for my glass, but Papa stopped me. He looked at the woman and said, "What's this?" Pointing to the sign directly behind her he said, "The sign says one glass of wine is two dollars. This is barely a half glass of wine." The woman said, "Oh, that's all we pour." Papa said, "The sign led me to believe I'd get one full glass of wine." She dismissively said, "Well, we only pour this amount."

Papa reached into his pocket and pulled out his wallet, quickly flipped it open and closed revealing a glimpse of his driver's license, and said, "I'm an inspector with the California Department of Weights and Measures. If a product says eight ounces, the contents of that product must contain eight ounces. This product is advertised as one full glass of wine, and you must provide us with a full glass of wine, or I have an obligation to report you for noncompliance."

I was dumbstruck. I couldn't believe he had the nerve to fabricate that fib on the spur-of-the-moment and deliver it with such bravado. The server immediately filled our glasses to the brim. He thanked her and as we walked away from the booth, she took down the sign. I was still speechless as Papa explained, "It makes me mad when people take advantage of consumers that way. It's unfair and that was the fastest way to stop it." He paused for a minute, and then said with a grin, "Did you see the look on her face?" I burst out laughing. I still can't believe he did that.

When Papa retired from his plumbing business, he continued to meet his business associates, clients, and friends for lunch. He enjoyed bringing a little cheer into the lives of people he interacted with each day—like bank tellers, postal workers, and grocery clerks. To each person he met he would say, "Do you know what you need today? A kiss!" Then, he'd slip his hand in his pocket, retrieve a Hershey's chocolate kiss, and present it to them. He loved the smiles he received in exchange for the candy kiss. He performed this ritual so often that when he walked through town people would ask, "Where is my kiss?" He kept a stash of kisses handy to avoid disappointing anyone.

Papa was a people person. He loved people. As my brother, Brad, said, "Papa knew how to engage people by making their interaction a positive, rewarding experience. People looked forward to seeing him, and he seldom disappointed."

Chapter 17

"Fantastic!"

PAPA SEEDED HIS PEARLS OF WISDOM AND LOVE as he interacted with us from day to day. They are a reflection of the life-lessons he learned, the power of positive thinking coupled with appropriate action, and the joy of living a full and abundant life. The simplicity of his words and actions are what make them so accessible. But the real secret to using them to improve your life or direct meaningful change is to believe in yourself and your ability to make it happen.

What I learned from Papa is that the first place to start is by saying aloud what you want until you're convinced that you deserve the best life has to offer, no matter what anyone else tells you. That statement of faith provides the momentum to propel you forward toward your goals and aspirations. Papa did that as a matter of routine.

My mom, Jan, recently sent this email to me:

> "My hairdresser reminded me that what you say becomes what you believe. I was reminded that your father always told people that his life, his company, his children, his wife, and his health were the best. People made a point

to tell me that they had never heard a man say so many wonderful things about his wife. They look at me with wonder because he said such nice things about me. His beliefs made him happy, and that seemed to be his goal."

Her remembrance was confirmed by Papa's granddaughter, Anna, who wrote, "Papa always said, 'I have the best house, best children, best wife, best job, best business, and best grandkids ever.' Everything was always the best (even if it wasn't), but by saying it out loud he manifested it—and everyone else believed it along with him."

Papa continually vocalized what he believed and wanted for himself and his family. In addition to all of "Papa's Pearls" that I've shared with you so far, here are some other things I heard him say more than once throughout the years . . .

"I'm a lucky guy. I always win."

Once, at a plumbing contractor's picnic, Papa bought a raffle ticket. He showed me the ticket and said, "This is a winning ticket. See those numbers? Those are winners. I'm a lucky guy. I always win." When the raffle drawing was over, Papa had won four tickets for primo seats to a San Francisco Giant's baseball game. It was uncanny how often he won raffle prizes and drawings.

Papa's granddaughter, Katie, recalled that whenever she invited Papa to church and school fundraisers where there was a raffle, he would say, "I don't want to enter that raffle because I'll win." She said, "It taught me to really evaluate if I wanted the excitement of winning some cheap-o thing just because it was there, or if I really wanted or needed it."

Papa's reputation for being lucky was well known in his circle of friends and business associates (probably, in no small part, from his self-promotion as a lucky guy). He went to lunch frequently with his buddies at a local bar and grill, and they shook dice to determine who would pay for the meal. Papa was one of the high rollers and rarely paid for lunch.

When I was twenty-seven, our family and a group of friends went on a horseback trail ride. At the end of the ride everyone dismounted. There were piles of horse manure in the yard and several people were complaining about the smell while dodging the piles as they walked to the barn. Papa pointed to a dried-out horse patty, tapped it with his boot and said, "What are you worried about? If you step in horse shit, it's good luck. I've stepped in it, and I'm lucky." What happened next was nothing short of bizarre. Every single person, including the trail master and a couple of complete strangers, walked over and purposely stepped on the horse patty by Papa's boot hoping for a little luck. Papa watched them all with an amused twinkle in his eye. He knew it wasn't the horse patty, it was believing his own words, "I'm lucky," that gave Papa the advantage.

"You can do anything you want to do if you set your mind to it."

Papa imparted this little gem to my sister, brother, and me as he rubbed our backs on school mornings, and he also shared it with his grandchildren as Anna revealed when she wrote, "Papa always used to tell us you can do anything you want to do if you set your mind to it! Boy, did I take that to heart and believe it! I have believed all my life that the world is truly mine! I can do anything I want to do, if I put my mind to it. I think that in this life, people sometimes don't do as much because they limit their own possibilities. I actually got into an argument in college with friends who said I couldn't any longer do anything I wanted. They said because we were in college, we had chosen our career paths and time was not in our favor anymore. I remember thinking how foolish they were! We debated and everyone was against me. I still hold true that we can do anything we want to do. I could still become a doctor or an astronaut or president: the world is always open. And what a gift Papa gave through this pearl. Look what he did with his life! Living proof! Thanks, Papa!"

"I can feel it, something really BIG is coming my way."

During his life, Papa would have what seemed like premonitions and he'd announce out loud, "I can feel it, something really BIG is coming my way." It usually resulted in an unexpected business deal, real estate transaction, or some kind of an income-producing opportunity. Whether he was intuitive, expressing his desire, or staking a claim out loud to the universe—he expected good fortune, believed he would get it, and gratefully received it.

"Oogie boogies!"

Papa would occasionally pause, look at you, and say, "Oogie boogies!" There was no particular rhyme or reason to it. It was a silly expression to let you know something exciting was in the air. As his granddaughter, Katie, explains, "Papa said 'oogie boogies' a little secretively and excitedly. It always meant something good was coming, be it a slice of pie or an unexpected gift. I like that he had a code word just to let you know you were in on something special. Calling out something good somehow makes it better. Sharing that something good is coming makes a memory not just a gift."

"Fantastic!"

Papa was nicknamed "Mr. Fantastic" by the tellers at his local bank. They called him that because whenever they asked him how he was, he always answered, "Fantastic!" In fact, for over sixty years, if a friend, a family member, or a complete stranger asked Papa, "How are you," his robust and heartfelt reply was, *"Fantastic!"*

He didn't say, "fine," "okay," "alright," "so-so," or "not bad." He always said with convincing enthusiasm, "Fantastic!" Some people were taken aback by it. They wondered, "How come you're not 'fine' like all the rest of us?"

His response to the question, "How are you," reinforced what he wanted for himself—to have a fantastic life. And it worked for him.

How about you? Do you want to have a fantastic life? Then start now, by affirming out loud what you want and expect. What will you say the next time someone asks, "How are you?"

Papa would say, "Fantastic!"

Epilogue

ON FATHER'S DAY, JUNE 19, 2011, I told Papa I was writing this book to share the pearls of wisdom he imparted to his children and grandchildren with many other people. After reading a rough draft to him, his eyes welled up with tears and with a raspy voice he said, "I think this is a good idea. You gotta tell 'em. This world . . ." His voice choked and trailed off as he shook his head sadly from side to side. Then, determined to finish his thought, he said softly, "They don't know. They don't know they're loved. You gotta tell 'em they're loved. And tell 'em to say it out loud every day to their families. 'You're loved.'" Then, regaining his composure Papa said, "I love you. You know that, right?"

I love you too, Papa. Forever.

About the Author

DIANE FLYNN KEITH IS FIRST AND FOREMOST PAPA'S DAUGHTER. She was born and raised on the San Francisco Peninsula. She and her husband Cliff live in Redwood City, California, where they reared their two sons, Nick and Chad.

Diane is an alternative education specialist, parenting coach, and author of the popular book, *Carschooling: Over 350 Entertaining Games & Activities To Turn Travel Time Into Learning Time.*

Diane is the co-author of two books, *Learning with Little Lulu Lemon*, and *Home Preschool Curriculum.* She has contributed to four books on the topic of homeschooling including, *The Homeschooling Almanac, The California Homeschool Guide, The Ultimate Book of Homeschooling Ideas*, and *Homeschooling Styles.*

Diane is recognized nationally and internationally as an expert in education outside the traditional classroom walls. She coaches thousands of parents through her writing, private consultations, speaking engagements, and websites that include:

- PapasPearls.com
- Homefires.com
- Carschooling.com

- ClickSchooling.com
- UniversalPreschool.com

She publishes three e-newsletters that include *ClickSchooling, Carschooling*, and *Universal Preschool*.

To help parents and children reach their full potential and enjoy the extraordinary lives they deserve, Diane is sharing the wit, wisdom, and loving heart of her father through her book, *Papa's Pearls: A Father's Gift of Love and Wisdom to His Children and Grandchildren*.

You'll find contact information for Diane Flynn Keith at www.PapasPearls.com.